Author's Biography

Peter Tatchell has written and campaigned extensively for lesbian and gay rights in the European context; contributing to the development of European strategies for homosexual equality and to the strengthening of lesbian and gay solidarity across national boundaries.

His contribution spans more than two decades. In 1973, Peter Tatchell represented the London Gay Liberation Front at the World Youth Festival in East Berlin. Smuggling thousands of lesbian and gay rights leaflets into East Germany, he was assaulted and interrogated after he staged a series of protests against homophobia in the Communist bloc.

More recently, Peter Tatchell was a delegate to the Helsinki Citizen's Assembly in Prague in 1990; co-drafting the homosexual rights declaration agreed by the Human Rights Commission.

Playing a leading role in lobbying the European Parliament, Peter Tatchell has helped secure its adoption of resolutions in support of lesbian and gay equality.

In 1991, he lodged a formal complaint against the European Commission. His complaint argued that by failing to ensure non-discrimination against homosexual people, the Commission was violating its Treaty obligations to ensure equality and fundamental freedoms for all citizens.

Peter Tatchell is also the author of *The Battle for Bermondsey* (Heretic Books 1983), *Democratic Defence* (GMP 1985) and *AIDS: A Guide to Survival* (3rd edn., GMP 1990).

EUROPE IN THE PINK

LESBIAN & GAY EQUALITY
IN THE NEW EUROPE

PETER TATCHELL

GMP

First published in March 1992 by GMP Publishers Ltd
P O Box 247, London N17 9QR, England

World Copyright © 1992 Peter Tatchell

A CIP catalogue record for this book
is available from the British Library

ISBN 0 85449 158 9

Distributed in North America by InBook
P O Box 120470, East Haven, CT 06512, USA

Distributed in Australia by Bulldog Books
P O Box 155, Broadway, NSW 2007, Australia

Front cover photographs:
top – Della Grace from her book
Love Bites (Éditions Aubrey Walter 1991)
bottom – Yves Paradis from his book
Joie de Vivre (Éditions Aubrey Walter 1991)

Printed and bound in the EC on environmentally-friendly paper
by Nørhaven A/S, Viborg, Denmark

Dedication

This book is dedicated to the many lesbian and gay activists in the countries of Eastern Europe who, often clandestinely and always courageously, have worked for homosexual emancipation — both during the period of Communist dictatorship and since the democratic revolutions of 1989.

In particular, it is dedicated to Peter Ambrus in Hungary, Jan Lany in Czechoslovakia, Lillian Kotter in Estonia, Ryszard Kisiel and Slawek Starosta in Poland, Roman Kalinin and Olga Zhuk in Russia, and Michael Eggart, Karsten Friedel, Christian Pulz, Uschi Sillge and Eduard Stapel in eastern Germany.

Their brave and determined efforts, frequently in conditions of great adversity, have not only advanced the human rights of lesbian and gay people. They have also strengthened and diversified the democratic culture of their societies; thereby helping to undermine the power and legitimacy of the totalitarian state and adding to the sum total of rights and freedoms enjoyed by their fellow citizens.

'I don't believe that progressive social change will come about through purely national efforts. There is a growing trend towards the globalization of politics, including more power being transferred to the European level. The political future increasingly lies with these European institutions and wider international forums... The lesbian and gay movement has to be there, at the centre of these newly-emerging power structures, if it wants to get our demands accepted'.

— *Herman Verbeek, MEP* (Green Left, Netherlands), the only openly gay Member of the European Parliament.

Acknowledgements

Europe in the Pink is a major update and expansion of my *Out in Europe* booklet which was published by Channel Four Television in 1990 to coincide with the lesbian and gay series, *Out on Tuesday*.

It also incorporates and develops many of the ideas on European strategies for lesbian and gay equality which I first expounded in articles in *Capital Gay, Changes, Gay Times, The Pink Paper, Rouge* and *Tribune*.

Information in the guide to lesbian and gay rights in the different European countries is based on my own researches through the London embassies, government press offices, and Ministries of Justice in the countries concerned; and on material supplied by civil liberties and homosexual rights organizations throughout Europe.

In addition, I have drawn on the researches of the following people to whom I am much indebted: Casimir Elsen, Helmut Graupner, Kurt Krickler, Rob Tielman, Evert van der Veen, and Kees Waaldijk. Their researches are published in the following key texts from which I have drawn information:

- *Report on the Legal Situation of Homosexual Men & Women in the Armed Forces,* by Casimir Elsen, published by the International Lesbian & Gay Association Information Pool on Gays & Lesbians and the Military, Belgium (1987).
- *Second ILGA Pink Book – A Global View of Lesbian & Gay Liberation and Oppression,* edited by Rob Tielman and Evert van der Veen, published by the Gay and Lesbian Studies Department of the University of Utrecht, Netherlands (1988).
- 'Strafrechtsvergleich zur Homosexualität im Europa', in *Diskussionsgrundlagen und Dokumente zur Homosexualität im Österreichischen Strafrecht,* by Helmut Graupner and Kurt Krickler, published by Homosexuelle Initiative Wien, Austria (1989).

- *The Iceberg Report – The ILGA Project to Uncover & Combat Discrimination in Europe,* edited by Kees Waaldijk, published by the Gay and Lesbian Studies Department of the University of Utrecht, Netherlands (1990).

In compiling the guide to lesbian and gay rights in Europe, I frequently encountered conflicting information from different sources. In such cases, the information has been carefully rechecked and reassessed. What is documented in *Europe in the Pink* is, to the best of my knowledge, correct at the time of going to press.

As well as those people I have already mentioned, I would also like to thank the following for their encouragement and assistance in making this book possible:

Peter Ashman of Justice; Tim Barnett and Anya Palmer of the Stonewall Group; David Bridle and Ben Summerskill of *The Pink Paper;* John Clark, David Murphy, Lisa Power and Nigel Warner of the International Lesbian and Gay Association; Jeremy Clarke and Philip Derbyshire of the Gay London Policing Group; David Fernbach, my editor at GMP; Kevin Flack of the London office of the British Labour Group of MEPs; Glyn Ford, Stephen Hughes and Carole Tongue, Labour MEPs; Phil Greasley and Maggie Holgate of Lesbian & Gay Employment Rights; Derek Jones of Channel Four Television; Peter Kent-Baguley of *Rouge* magazine; Colin Kotz of the administrative secretariat of the Socialist Group of MEPs in the European Parliament; Labour MPs Harry Cohen, Dawn Primarolo, Gavin Strang, Audrey Wise and the late Allan Roberts; John Marshall and David Smith of *Gay Times,* Michael Mason and Andrew Saxton of *Capital Gay;* Willemien Ruygrok of the Dutch lesbian and gay organization COC; Olli Stalstrom of the Finnish homosexual rights organization SETA; and Jon Voss of the Swedish gay newspaper, *Reporter.*

CONTENTS

A Guide to Lesbian & Gay Rights in Europe

Appendices

Introduction

All of Europe is in a process of momentous change. The Cold War is over. A wave of democratic revolutions has swept Eastern Europe. New nations are emerging as old empires break down. The European Community (EC) is accelerating the process of economic and political union.

Out of this radical reshaping of borders, alliances, ideologies and social systems, a common European identity and consciousness is beginning to emerge. It is, perhaps, best summed up in Mikhail Gorbachev's vision of a 'common European home' embracing all the peoples of Europe, from the Atlantic to the Urals. Already, there are signs that the EC could be the foundation of this united Europe if, as expected, it eventually opens up its membership to all the nations of Europe, East and West.

Developments in the direction of a united Europe involve both dangers and opportunities. On the one hand, they present the danger of a new European chauvinism leading to an authoritarian and nationalistic 'Fortress Europe'. On the other hand, there is the opportunity of a new European enlightenment based on a commitment to military disarmament, environmental protection, social equality, human rights and global justice.

The future character of a united Europe has big implications for the lesbian and gay communities. Will we win or lose from closer European integration? Can a united Europe be a means for the continent-wide advancement of lesbian and gay equality? Would the harmonization of laws result in our civil rights being reduced to the level of the most backward countries or uplifted to the standards of the most progressive?

It is clear that European integration may affect different lesbian and gay communities in different ways. Black and Asian homosexuals are likely to be particularly adversely affected. EC proposals for common citizenship and visa laws could mean that non-EC lesbians and gay men, who can currently live and work legally in the Community, may face new restrictions on their entry into the EC, their civic rights and their freedom of internal movement. Plans for tough new regulations on immigration and political asylum could make it harder for lesbians and gay men fleeing persecution in their home countries to get refugee status in the EC. They may also mean that non-EC lesbians and gay men who have relationships with EC nationals could find it more difficult to get residence rights to settle with their partners.

Whatever our misgivings about particular aspects of closer European co-operation, the trend towards a united Europe is an unmistakable fact. It is happening whether we like it or not. What's forcing the pace of EC integration is a mixture of high-minded idealism and low-down self-interest. Big business argues that the only way the countries of Europe can compete with the United States and Japan is by merging their economic power. This 'Europeanization' of capital is rendering the individual nation-states of Europe increasingly redundant.

In contrast, liberal opinion argues, more altruistically that we live in an interdependent world facing common threats, such as toxic pollution and global warming, which can only be overcome by joint endeavour. Hence the need for the European nations to co-operate for their mutual survival.

We can therefore no more halt the development of a united Europe than those who, last century, sought to stop the merger of the principalities which led to the creation of the modern states of Germany and Italy. We can, however, adapt the unification process to our advantage and influence the character of the new Europe in a progressive direction. Through political alliances and campaigns it is possible, indeed essential, to ensure that lesbian and gay equality is an integral part of a united Europe. The political project of winning 'Equality in Europe' is going to become increasingly important in years to come, as more and more of the decisions which affect our lives are taken at the European level.

This book is not a defence or celebration of Europe as it is, but a vision of what it could be: a democratic United States of Europe which respects the human rights of all people everywhere, including lesbians and gay men.

THE EUROPEAN
RECORD SO FAR

European Community

The European Community (EC) comprises 12 countries with a combined population of 320 million people — Belgium, Denmark, France, Germany, Greece, Ireland, Italy, Luxemburg, Netherlands, Portugal, Spain and the United Kingdom. These countries account for nearly 90 per cent of the population of Western Europe. They include an estimated 32 million lesbians and gay men, and 48 million bisexual people.[1]

The EC consists of three main institutions:

- *The European Parliament* — It is made up of 518 directly-elected Members of the European Parliament from the 12 member states. Despite being the only democratically elected EC body, it is relatively powerless. With no authority to initiate legislation, it has little more than a consultative and advisory role in relation to the more powerful European Commission and Council of Ministers.
- *The European Commission* — The equivalent of a high-powered executive civil service and policy think-tank, it is administered by 17 commissioners appointed by the governments of each member state. The Commission is responsible for proposing legislation and implementing the decisions of the Council of Ministers.
- *The Council of Ministers* — Composed of 12 Ministers representing each of the national governments of the member states, it is the main policy-making and legislative institution of the EC. However, it meets in secret and many of its key decisions require unanimity. Able to over-rule the Parliament and the Commission, the Council is the ultimate seat of power.

The legal powers of the EC and its various institutions are set out in the EC Treaties — principally the Treaty of Rome which led to the establishment of the EC in 1957, and the Single European Act which amended that Treaty in 1986.

The EC was originally set up as an 'economic community' and is still primarily concerned with economic matters. However, since the passage of the Single European Act, it has begun to take on a slightly broader social agenda. This has encouraged attempts by Members of the European Parliament (MEPs) to promote policies in support of lesbian and gay rights. These have included proposals in 1985 for the commemoration of the homosexual victims of Nazism, and condemnation of the British government's prohibition on the promotion of homosexuality under Section 28 in 1988.

Most significantly, in March 1984, the European Parliament adopted the recommendations of the Squarcialupi Report *On Sexual Discrimination in the Workplace*,[2] which was prepared under the sponsorship of the Italian Communist MEP Vera Squarcialupi. Deploring anti-homosexual discrimination and recommending equal rights for lesbians and gay men, the Parliament urged the EC member states to:

- Abolish laws against consenting sexual relations between people of the same sex.
- Introduce an equal age of consent for heterosexuals and homosexuals.
- Ban the keeping of special records on lesbians and gay men by the police and other authorities.
- Reject the classification of homosexuality as a mental illness.

The Parliament also called on the Commission to submit proposals to outlaw discrimination in the workplace on the grounds of a person's sexuality, and to draw up a report on all aspects of discrimination against lesbians and gay men in the member states.

At the time, this report was welcomed by the then Social Affairs Commissioner, Ivor Richards, who acknowledged that discrimination against lesbians and gay men was 'unacceptable'.

He told MEPs that, on the basis of Articles 100 and 117 of the EC Treaties, the Commission planned to recommend new legislation on unfair dismissals. With the use of additional powers under Article 235, he suggested this legislation could possibly be extended to include job protection for lesbians and gay men.[3]

However, despite these assurances, the Squarcialupi Report was never acted upon by the Commission and the Council of Ministers. According to the Dutch lesbian activist, Willemien Ruygrok: 'On many occasions, we wrote to the European Commission asking them what they were doing to implement the Squarcialupi Report. Most of the times we got no answer. The other times, they were always evasive'.[4]

Despite this inaction, the European Parliament has reiterated its commitment to lesbian and gay equality in four further reports and resolutions since 1984:

- The D'Ancona Report *On Violence Against Women* (June 1986) called 'for the extension of the concept of non-discrimination...to cover both discrimination on the basis of sex or marital status and discrimination on the basis of sexual preference'.[5]

- The Parodi Report *On the Fight Against Aids* (May 1989) urged the Member States and the Commission to ensure 'compliance with existing laws and measures against discrimination on the grounds of race, sex, sexual orientation etc'.[6]

- The Buron Report *On the Community Charter of the Fundamental Social Rights of Workers* — The Social Charter (November 1989) included the commitment 'that priority should be given in the Charter and the action programme to...the right of all workers to equal protection regardless of their nationality, race, religion, age, sex, sexual preference or legal status'.[7]

- The Ford Report *On Racism and Xenophobia* (October 1990) proposed that 'a convention be drafted on a common refugee and asylum policy building on the principles of the UN Convention on Refugees allowing all those threatened by persecution because of their political, religious or philosophical beliefs or convictions, or gender or sexual orientation, to benefit'.[8]

As with the Squarcialupi Report, these four recommendations from the European Parliament were completely ignored by the Commission and the Council of Ministers. The Commission argued that the EC Treaties restrict what it is legally empowered to do. Since there is nothing explicit in the EC Treaties about the rights of lesbians and gay men, the Commission insisted it has no legal competence to take action on matters of sexuality.[9]

Since 1990, however, faced with concerted lobbying from the lesbian and gay movement and sympathetic MEPs in the European Parliament, the Commission has hinted at a possible change of attitude.

At a meeting of the Social Affairs Committee of the European Parliament in January 1990, the British Labour MEP Stephen Hughes argued that discrimination against lesbians and gay men is an impediment to the goal of creating a barrier-free internal market, as set out in Article 100a of the EC Treaties. He suggested that homosexual people would not feel free to take up employment offers in other EC countries which tolerated anti-gay discrimination. Hughes went on to urge the President of the European Commission, Jacques Delors, to remedy this obstacle to the free movement of persons by bringing forward proposals — under the Action Programme on the Social Charter — to outlaw discrimination in employment on the grounds of sexual orientation. Delors responded by acknowledging that discrimination does constitute a barrier to the achievement of a common market, and that Article 100a does give the EC power to act against discrimination. He indicated that the Commission would consider the introduction of new legislation to tackle discrimination; though he didn't specify whether this would include a ban on discrimination against homosexuals.[10]

The same month, Andre-Guy Kirchberger, a senior official in the cabinet of the Social Affairs Commissioner, Vasso Papandreou, admitted that the EC was under pressure to introduce measures to protect lesbians and gay men in the workplace. He confirmed that Article 235 of the EC Treaties gives the Commission 'discretionary powers to act on matters which, although not specified in the Treaties, conform to the general objectives of the EC'. This could provide a legal basis for legislation against homophobia in employment, according to Kirchberger. 'Discrimination against homosexuals is an issue we haven't dealt with before...but it will have to be addressed', he conceded.[11]

Evidence of tensions and contradictions within the Commission over how to respond to demands for lesbian and gay equality surfaced in February 1990. Mrs Daniela Napoli, the administrator responsible for human rights issues in the office of the Secretariat-General of the Commission, declared: 'It is unacceptable that workers should suffer discrimination on account of their private lives or conduct, which includes their sexual preference'. However, she went on to insist that the Commission has no legal power to outlaw anti-homosexual discrimination. It's a matter for the national governments of the EC countries, and the Commission cannot over-ride 'the laws and values contained in the cultural traditions of the different member states', she said. Responding to queries as to why the Commission had never produced a report on homophobic discrimination within the EC, as requested by the European Parliament in 1984, Napoli pleaded that it was due to 'administrative and financial constraints'.[12]

Later the same month, a more sympathetic reception was given to a joint delegation of representatives from the International Lesbian and Gay Association and the British lesbian and gay organization, the Stonewall Group. They met Andre-Guy Kirchberger in Brussels to press for EC action against homosexual inequality. Though Kirchberger didn't offer any specific pledges, he did suggest that it might be feasible to adapt certain parts of the Social Charter to meet the needs of lesbians and gay men. He also acknowledged that discrimination against homosexuals could be construed as contradicting the EC's goal of creating an obstacle-free internal market. It could be argued, he admitted, that EC-wide employment protection legislation was necessary to allow lesbians and gay men to move freely around the Community without fear of discrimination. Kirchberger again reiterated that Article 235 of the EC Treaties might provide a plausible legal basis for future legislation for lesbian and gay equality. He concluded by requesting the Stonewall

Group to compile a dossier on anti-homosexual discrimination in the member states, and on the implications of the creation of the Single Market for the lesbian and gay communities.[13]

In April 1990, the Stonewall Group presented a dossier along these lines to the Commission. Entitled *Harmonization Within the European Community – The Reality for Lesbians & Gay Men*, it argued that the widely variable levels of discrimination and protection for homosexuals in the different member states undermine the Commission's commitment to the harmonization of regulations and constitute a barrier to the free movement of people – contrary to the goals set out in the EC Treaties. It went on to document some of the possible adverse consequences of the post-1992 Single European Market for lesbians and gay men, including the following examples:

- A Greek gay man who takes advantage of the improved mobility of labour to seek employment in Ireland would risk imprisonment if he has sex with another man because homosexuality is still totally illegal in Ireland.
- A Danish lesbian whose relationship with another woman is legally recognized in Denmark would lose that legal recognition if she was posted to her company's Portuguese subsidiary following the liberalization of business operations under the internal market (Portuguese law doesn't recognize same-sex partnerships).

The Stonewall dossier concluded by calling for EC action under the Social Charter to eliminate anti-gay discrimination; citing the Charter's commitment to 'combat every form of discrimination...in order to ensure equal treatment'. In particular, it urged EC-wide legislation against the refusal of employment, denial of compassionate leave, harassment at work and dismissal or demotion on the grounds of sexuality.

Simultaneously, other British-based lesbian and gay organizations lobbied the Commission. The Campaign for Homosexual Equality wrote to the Social Affairs Commissioner, Vasso Papandreou, urging 'support for equality and non-discrimination for the lesbian and gay citizens of the EC'. Similar sentiments were expressed by the Organization for Lesbian & Gay Action, which called for the Social Charter to be amended to include a commitment to 'non-discrimination on the grounds of sexual preference'. Lesbian & Gay Employment Rights (LAGER) argued that anti-homosexual discrimination in the workplace is a waste of human resources and a restriction on free competition, often denying employers the opportunity to take on the best person for the job when that person happens to be lesbian or gay. This discrimination could, suggested LAGER, hinder the free movement of lesbian and gay people by discouraging them from taking up job offers in EC countries where inequality is tolerated and unchecked by legal protection.

In May 1990, during Question Time in the European Parliament, the British Labour MEP Glyn Ford called on the Commission to acknowledge that discrimination against lesbians and gay men was 'a disincentive and an obstacle' to the achievement of three key objectives of the EC: the free movement of people, the creation of a barrier-free internal market, and the harmonization of the laws of the member states. Ford argued that these objectives are set out in Articles 48, 49, 100, 100a, and 101 of the EC Treaties, and that they therefore provide a legal basis for action against homosexual inequality in the workplace. Replying on behalf of the Commission, Jacques Delors said it had 'no powers to intervene in possible cases of discrimination by member states against sexual minorities'. He recommended that the European Convention on Human Rights was a more appropriate means of tackling such discrimination.[14]

The Commission's reversion to a hard-line position shocked many MEPs who'd been expecting a more sympathetic response. Stephen Hughes, MEP, condemned the 'twists and turns' in official EC attitudes, but took comfort from the supportive noises coming from senior officials in Vasso Papandreou's cabinet.

Indeed, not long afterwards, continued patient lobbying resulted in EC legislation banning the keeping of secret files concerning a person's 'sexual life'. Article 17 of the EC directive on The Protection of Individuals in Relation to the Processing of Personal Data, agreed in 1990, stated: 'The member states shall prohibit the automatic processing of data revealing ethnic or racial origin, political opinions, religious or philosophical beliefs or trade union membership, and of data concerning health or sexual life, without the express and written consent, freely given, of the data subject'.[15]

An even bigger breakthrough came in December 1990 when the first ever meeting between the Social Affairs Commissioner, Vasso Papandreou, and an EC-wide delegation of lesbian and gay organizations took place. Arising from this meeting, Papandreou undertook to:

- Appoint a senior official with formal responsibility for homosexual issues and liaison.
- Fund a report on the impact of the Single European Market on lesbians and gay men.
- Propose that the forthcoming Code of Practice on sexual harassment would include the recommendation that employees be protected against harassment on the grounds of sexuality.[16]

As a result of this latter pledge, in 1991 the Commission's Code of Practice, Protecting the Dignity of Women & Men at Work, declared: 'It is undeniable that harassment on the grounds of sexual orientation undermines the dignity at work of those affected and it is impossible to regard such harassment as appropriate workplace behaviour'.[17] Though this Code of Practice was only a recommendation, and did not have the force of law, it was, nevertheless, a historic breakthrough. For the first time ever, the EC had explicitly included 'sexual orientation' within its anti- discrimination policies.

While the EC is now showing signs of a greater willingness to take on board lesbian and gay equality issues, its alleged lack of legal competence on these issues remains the main stumbling block to further progress. The Commission's powers are governed by the EC Treaties. It argues that since there's nothing in these Treaties about homosexual rights, it therefore has no legal authority to legislate against anti-gay discrimination. Such a view is based on a very narrow and illiberal interpretation of the EC Treaties. Ultimately, of course, the attitudes of the Commission and the Council of Ministers are questions of political will and policy priorities. Currently, they see lesbian and gay equality as too controversial. They also treat it as a low priority compared with the completion of the Single European Market, plans for economic and monetary union, and other preoccupying issues such as nationalist unrest in Eastern Europe and economic aid to the ex-Soviet republics.

To challenge this inaction, on 1 July 1991, the author of this book lodged a formal complaint against the EC, accusing it of ignoring the rights of lesbians and gay men and pursuing policies of exclusion and discrimination. The 56-page, 14,000-word complaint was submitted with the backing of the civil liberties watchdog, Liberty, and of British Labour MEPs. The first ever human rights complaint submitted through the London offices of the European Commission, the document argued that, by failing to take action against homosexual inequality, the EC was violating its legal obligations under its Treaties. These require it to promote freedom, equality and fundamental rights for all EC citizens.[18]

1   These estimates are based on sex surveys which suggest that ten per cent of the population is predominantly or exclusively lesbian or gay, and that a further 15 per cent are bisexual.

2   *Official Journal of the European Communities*, No. C 104, 16. 4. 1984, p. 46-48.

3   *Debates of the European Parliament*, No. 1-311, 13 March 1984, p. 17.

4   *The Pink Paper*, 12 May 1990.

5   *Official Journal of the European Communities*, No. C 176, 14. 7. 1986, p. 75.

6   *Official Journal of the European Communities*, No. C 158, 26. 6. 1989, p. 479-80.

7   *Official Journal of the European Communities*, No. C 323, 27. 12. 1989, p. 46.

8   European Parliament Session Documents, A3-195/90, PE 141.205/fin, 23. 7. 1990, p. 159, approved as recorded in the *Minutes of Proceedings of the European Parliament*, 10. 10. 1990, p. 3.

9   Jacques Delors, 29 November 1988, reply to Written Questions Nos. 633/88 and 958/88 tabled by Ernest Glinne, MEP.

10 *Capital Gay*, 26 January 1990.

11 *Gay Times*, April 1990.

12 *Capital Gay*, 30 March 1990.
13 *Capital Gay*, 16 February 1990 and *Gay Times*, March 1990.
14 Answer to Oral Question H-594/90 tabled by Glyn Ford, MEP (Doc EN/QO/88726).
15 *Official Journal of the European Communities*, No. C 277, 5. 11. 1990, p. 9.
16 *Capital Gay*, 11 January 1991.
17 *Capital Gay*, 13 December 1991.
18 *Gay Times*, August 1991.

Council of Europe

Founded in 1949, the 26-nation Council of Europe is the oldest pan-European institution. It's separate from the European Community (EC). Unlike the EC, it is not primarily concerned with economic issues. Instead, the Council of Europe's principle aims are the promotion of parliamentary democracy and human rights through the Europe-wide agreement of conventions on issues such as data protection and the prevention of torture. Its membership includes all the democratic states in Western Europe: the EC countries, the nations of the European Free Trade Association, and the non-aligned and neutral states. More recently, it has admitted the new East European democracies of Czechoslovakia, Hungary and Poland.

Decision-making power within the Council of Europe resides with the Committee of Ministers which consists of the Foreign Ministers of the 26 member states. They are empowered to approve conventions and make policy recommendations to the national governments. In addition, there is a Parliamentary Assembly made up of MPs from the national parliaments of each country. However, the Assembly's role is purely advisory. Though influential, it lacks legislative authority.

In October 1981, the Parliamentary Assembly adopted Recommendation 924 which urged the legalization of homosexuality, common ages of consent for heterosexuals and homosexuals, equality of treatment for homosexuals in the workplace, the abolition of police files on homosexuals, and the right of homosexual parents to have access to and custody of their children without restriction on the grounds of their sexual orientation. It also agreed with Resolution 756 which affirmed that all individuals have 'the right to sexual self-determination', condemned as having 'no sound scientific or medical basis' the theory that homosexuality is a mental disturbance, and called on the World Health Organization to 'delete homosexuality from its International Classification of Diseases'.

Recommendation 924 and Resolution 756 were milestones in the struggle for homosexual equality. Never before had a major international human rights organization condemned homophobic discrimination and called for the recognition and protection of the rights of lesbian and gay people. Alas, more than a decade later, these appeals for homosexual equality remain unheeded in many member states, including Britain.

The most famous and effective institution of the Council of Europe is the European Convention on Human Rights (ECHR). The ECHR is administered by the European Commission on Human Rights. It assesses appeals against breaches of the ECHR and rules on whether they are admissible for consideration. Those that are accepted, then go forward to the European Court of Human Rights for judgement. The ECHR doesn't include any explicit commitments to the human rights of lesbians and gay men. However, on two occasions, it has been interpreted to recommend that Britain and Ireland repeal their total ban on male homosexual relations.

In 1981, following an appeal by Jeffrey Dudgeon, the European Court of Human Rights ruled that the criminalization of all consenting homosexual relationships in Northern Ireland was a violation of a person's right to privacy, contrary to Article 8 of the ECHR. As a result, the British government was forced to legalize homosexuality in Northern Ireland in 1982.[1]

On similar grounds, arising from a case brought by David Norris, in 1988 the European Court of Human Rights ruled that the Irish prohibition on all homosexual acts was illegal (also citing Article 8). This decision is expected to lead to law reform in Ireland in the near future.[2]

However, as well as these successful appeals to the ECHR, there have also been several cases where the European Commission on Human Rights has turned down challenges to discriminatory anti-homosexual laws. There have been five unsuccessful attempts by British lesbians and gay men to use the ECHR mechanisms since the early 1980s:

- In 1981, John Bruce, a gay member of the armed forces, appealed against the discriminatory ban on service personnel having any form of same-sex relationship.
- The following year, there was an attempt to overturn the discriminatory age of consent laws by a gay teenager, Richard Desmond.
- In 1983, Martin Johnson used the ECHR to challenge the discriminatory sexual offences and privacy laws which allowed the police to raid a gay birthday party in a private house and arrest all the guests.
- The case brought by Mary Simpson in 1985 sought to reverse the discriminatory housing laws which, in the event of a council tenant's death, gives a surviving heterosexual partner the right to inherit the tenancy, but denies the same right to the surviving partner of a homosexual relationship.
- In 1986, an anonymous gay man tried to challenge the discriminatory immigration regulations which deny a foreign citizen who has a committed relationship with a British gay person the right to immigrate and take up residence in the UK with their partner.

All five of these appellants failed to get a favourable ruling from the European Commission of Human Rights. In the Desmond age of consent case, which was bought under Articles 8 and 14 of the ECHR, the Commission deferred to the right of each member state to fix its own minimum age for homosexual contacts. It ruled that in doing so each state was entitled to take into account the 'moral interests and welfare of young people'.[3]

This judgement showed up the weaknesses and limitations of the ECHR as a mechanism for the defence of lesbian and gay rights. Everything hinges on the interpretation of the various Articles. The ECHR contains no specific protection on the grounds of sexual orientation. Article 14 does, however, make it clear that the 'rights and freedoms set forth in this Convention shall be secured without discrimination on any ground such as sex, race, colour, language, religion, political or other opinion, national or social origin, association with a national minority, property, birth or other status'. The key principle of this Article is in opposition to discrimination 'on any ground'. The references to 'sex, race, colour' and so on are merely illustrative, but non-exhaustive, examples of this. Article 14 could thus be reasonably interpreted to include a commitment to non-discrimination in general and, by implication, to non-discrimination against lesbians and gay men. But it isn't. This is largely due to a lack of political will. Most member states deem homosexuality to be an issue which is too contentious to justify a liberal interpretation of Article 14.

For this reason, the International Lesbian and Gay Association (ILGA) is currently campaigning to get official consultative status with the Council of Europe in order to be able to more readily influence its deliberations. Its first application was rejected in 1990. The Council justified its rejection on the grounds it was not doing work around lesbian and gay issues.[4] Undaunted, ILGA is also seeking to secure the amendment of Article 14 to insert an explicit commitment that the ECHR's 'rights and freedoms' should apply without discrimination on the grounds of 'sexual orientation'. Ultimately, ILGA's goal is the enactment of a supplementary protocol to the ECHR to clearly recognize and explicitly protect the human rights of homosexuals. 'Simply amending Article 14 would probably not be sufficient', according to ILGA activist Nigel Warner. 'There's a need for a whole separate protocol to be added to the Convention which would spell-out in detail the right of lesbians and gay men to equality and non-discrimination'.[5] ILGA's campaign for a new protocol was launched in Copenhagen, in May 1990, at a meeting called to coincide with the Conference on Security and Co-operation in Europe's (CSCE) convention on human rights.[6]

Pressure for reforming the ECHR has been building up since 1982 when the Legal Affairs Committee of the Council of Europe sponsored a conference on criminal law and sexual behaviour. Two radical reports came out of this gathering. One, from the Director of the Institute of Criminology at Cambridge University, recommended that Article 14 should be amended to include sexual orientation. The other, by a West German judge, proposed that the member states should adopt a common age of consent of 14 for both heterosexuals and homosexuals.[7]

In 1990, the Non-Governmental Organizations which have consultative status with the Council of Europe urged the member states to repeal all discriminatory anti-gay laws and to actively 'fight' against homosexual inequality. They also called on the Council of Europe to monitor and report on infringements of the human rights of lesbians and gay men in the member countries.[8]

With all of Europe moving towards closer co-operation, it's probable that most of the newly-democratized countries of Eastern Europe will eventually join the Council of Europe. Czechoslovakia, Hungary and Poland have already become members. If the Council of Europe's membership is further broadened, it could become an increasingly important arena for the strengthening of human rights policies across the continent, including common policies for the advancement of equal rights for lesbian and gay people.

1 Lawrence R. Helfer, *Finding a Consensus on Equality: The Homosexual Age of Consent and the European Convention on Human Rights*, New York University Law Review, Volume 65, Number 4, October 1990, p. 1044-45 and 1059-61.

2 Ibid.

3 Ibid., p.1085.

4 *Capital Gay*, 7 September 1990.

5 *The Pink Paper*, 21 April 1990.

6 *Capital Gay*, 1 June 1990.

7 Lawrence R. Helfer, ibid., p. 1093-94.

8 *Capital Gay*, 12 October 1990.

Eastern Europe

So far as the formal legal status of lesbian and gay sexuality is concerned, the countries of Eastern Europe have often been more progressive than the West — even during the period of Communist rule. Of the eight East European countries, five have legalized same-sex relationships and in the former Yugoslavia so have three of the six republics. In Poland, the age of consent has been 15 for both heterosexuals and homosexuals since 1932. Czechoslovakia and Hungary decriminalized homosexuality in 1961. Even Albania introduced a common age of consent of 14 for everyone in 1977.

However, this formal legal enlightenment has usually not been matched by equality for lesbians and gay men in practice. Homophobic prejudice, police repression and the absence of lesbian and gay social venues and community organizations has been particularly acute in Albania, Bulgaria, Romania and the republics of the former Soviet Union (together with Romania, these ex-Soviet republics — with the exception of the Ukraine — still have a total ban on homosexual behaviour).

In the other East European countries, although official and public attitudes have been less homophobic, until the mid-1980s none of the Communist governments did anything to tackle anti-gay prejudice and discrimination, or to meet the needs of their lesbian and gay communities. There was no discussion about homosexuality in the state-controlled media or in sex education lessons in schools. Gay cafes and cruising areas were periodically raided. Same-sex partnerships went unrecognized. Lesbians and gay men were socially invisible. Their existence was shrouded by official silence and indifference. Indeed, the dominant unspoken attitude of the ruling governments was one of repressive tolerance. Homosexuality tended to be regarded as a lingering leftover from the distorted social relations of the capitalist past. In a perfected socialist society, lesbianism and gayness would, it was believed, eventually disappear. The result was that, outside of artistic and intellectual circles, homosexuals remained closeted and fearful of social ostracism and discrimination.

During the Communist era, one of the biggest obstacles to the advancement of lesbian and gay equality in the East European countries was the state ideology of the 'socialist family'. It was the cornerstone of Communist government policy for 40 years. Speaking prior to the overthrow of Communism, one East German gay activist, Christian Pulz, observed: 'The official policies of the state have always been constructed around the concept of the socialist family. Everything in our societies has been family-oriented...(This) means it is difficult to enact policies for the benefit of gay people if they contradict the pro-family policy of the state'. In Romania, under the Ceausescu regime, the ideology of the 'New Socialist Family' had particularly brutal consequences. Women were imprisoned for having abortions and homosexuals were subject to forced psychiatric treatment.

It was not until the 1980s, under the impact of the newly-emergent lesbian and gay movements and the revival of the tradition of scientific sexology, that official attitudes began to change in the East European countries. The new enlightened response was most pronounced in East Germany. It had a long history of radical sex research dating back to Dr Magnus Hirschfeld who founded the Institute for Sexual Science in Berlin in 1919. Reviving this progressive sexological tradition in the mid-1980s, East German sex researchers began to theorise that homosexuality is as natural for a minority of the population as heterosexuality is for the majority. Emphasizing a biologically-deterministic view of homosexuality, sex scientists such as Dr Edwin Gunther suggested that if homosexuality is a pre-given condition over which individuals have no control, it is scientifically and ethically wrong for lesbians and gay men to suffer prejudice and discrimination.[1]

This line of argument, together with the need to win the confidence of gay men to fight the Aids epidemic, convinced the old-guard Communist regime of Erich Honecker that it should remove legal inequalities and actively facilitate the social integration of lesbians and gay men. Accordingly, in 1989 East Germany lowered the age of consent for male homosexuals to 14 years, bringing it into line with the age for heterosexual men and women.

Earlier, in the mid-1980s, the East German government had authorized a series of positive articles about same-sex relationships in the Communist-controlled press, the provision of supportive counselling for homosexuals through the state-run marriage guidance councils, and the setting up of a network of lesbian and gay clubs within the official youth organizations.

Some lesbian and gay activists in East Germany were very critical of these reforms. They accused the Honecker government of being motivated not by a genuine commitment to homosexual equality, but by a cynical desire to buy-off lesbian and gay dissent and win the support of the homosexual community for a beleaguered and discredited Communist regime. These critics pointed out that the change in government attitudes towards homosexuals coincided with the increasingly assertive demands of the lesbian and gay movement and its growing alliance with other dissident social movements.

Founded in 1982, the contemporary East German lesbian and gay movement was initially illegal. It met under the auspices of the Protestant church, which was the only social institution independent of the state and the only forum for social opposition which the Communists dared not act against.

In 1986, the lesbian and gay movement received its first tacit official recognition when government representatives apologized for the brutal police suppression of attempts to lay 'pink triangle' wreaths at the sites of former concentration camps. They pledged that in future lesbian and gay organizations would be allowed to commemorate the homosexual victims of Nazism.[2]

Elsewhere in Eastern Europe at around the same time, a similar combination of enlightened sexology and an emergent lesbian and gay movement began to change government attitudes in Czechoslovakia, Hungary, Poland and Yugoslavia. The need to win the trust of the gay community to combat the spread of HIV was also a key factor which encouraged the Communists to begin liaising with their lesbian and gay communities. According to Hungarian activists: 'It was the appearance of Aids that made the association (with the government) possible. Combating Aids is the mutual interest that links (us)'.[3]

The development of lesbian and gay movements in several East European countries led to attempts to co-ordinate their efforts. On 8 November 1987, the 70th anniversary of the Bolshevik Revolution, the first unofficial and semi-clandestine conference of lesbian and gay activists in Eastern Europe took place in Budapest, Hungary. It was attended by 31 delegates representing lesbian and gay organizations in Czechoslovakia, East Germany, Hungary, Poland and Yugoslavia. The following year, 60 people attended the second conference which was held in Warsaw in the district headquarters of the Polish Communist Party.[4] In 1989, the third conference met in Budapest again. Convened in the newly-opened gay cultural centre, it was hosted by the Hungarian homosexual rights organization, Homeros Lambda. Since then, these annual conferences have gone from strength to strength — growing larger, going public and getting positive coverage in the mainstream press.

While lesbian and gay campaigners in Eastern Europe have been highly critical of the old Communist regimes, they are also apprehensive about what has, or might, replace them. In some countries, the democratic revolutions of late 1989 have greatly strengthened the influence of the Catholic and Orthodox churches and unleashed wave of right-wing nationalist movements. The appearance of neo-Fascist groups in eastern Germany and chauvinistic organizations, such as Pamyat, in Russia, with their ideologies of 'family, church and nation', have raised fears that the trend towards greater social acceptance of lesbians and gay men could be halted, or even put into reverse. Already in Poland the influence of the Catholic church on the Solidarity-led government has put a break on further initiatives for lesbian and gay equality. More ominously, at Warsaw University, the lesbian and gay group and the Aids helpline were evicted from the university student club in 1990 by the Solidarity-backed Student's Union. In the words of one Polish gay activist, Slawek Starosta: 'Sections of the old Communist regime were more sympathetic and supportive of lesbian and gay rights than many of the present people in Solidarity'.

On the positive side, the post-1989 democratization has led to the enactment of an equal age of consent of 15 in Czechoslovakia, the election of openly gay candidates in the former territory of East Germany, the insertion into the Slovenian draft constitution of an explicit guarantee of equal rights for lesbians and gay men, and the emergence of a high-profile Russian homosexual rights movement centred on the cities of Moscow and St Petersburg.

1   *Gay Times*, July 1987.
2   *Capital Gay*, 22 May 1987.
3   *The Pink Paper*, 19 May 1988.
4   Ibid.

Conference on Security & Co-operation in Europe

The Conference on Security and Co-operation in Europe (CSCE) is the only truly pan-European institution. It brings together all the nations of Europe, East and West; plus the US and Canada. It will embrace 50-plus countries when the ex-Soviet and ex-Yugoslav republics join. The CSCE holds periodic summits attended by the presidents and prime ministers of the member states. Decisions are taken by a negotiated consensus.

The CSCE's most outstanding achievement was the signing, in 1975, of the Helsinki Agreement on East-West co-operation. An international treaty binding on the signatory states, this Agreement sets out a wide-ranging remit for co-operation between all the countries of Europe with regard to industrial production, science and technology, trade and aid, environmental protection, cultural exchanges, education and training, common security and disarmament, and the protection of human rights.

The Helsinki Final Act (1 (a) VII), includes a strong commitment to uphold the human rights of all European citizens:

> 'The participating states will respect human rights and fundamental freedoms, including the freedom of thought, conscience, religion or belief, for all without distinction as to race, sex, language or religion. They will promote and encourage the effective use of civil, political, economic, social, cultural and other rights and freedoms, all of which derive from the inherent dignity of the human person and are essential for his free will and full development'.

The more recent Conference on the Human Dimension of the CSCE, held in Copenhagen in June 1990, reiterated these commitments. Article 5.9 of the final declaration stated:

> 'All persons are equal before the law and are entitled without any discrimination to the equal protection of the law. In this respect, the law will prohibit any discrimination and guarantee to all persons equal and effective protection against discrimination on any ground'.

This was followed up by the CSCE's Charter of Paris for a New Europe. Signed in November 1990, it pledged:

> 'Human rights and fundamental freedoms are the birthright of all human beings, are inalienable and are guaranteed by law. Their protection and promotion is the first responsibility of government...We affirm that, without discrimination, every individual has the right to: freedom of thought, conscience and religion or belief; freedom of expression...We express our determination to combat all forms of racial and ethnic hatred, anti-semitism, xenophobia and discrimination against anyone'.

Though there is nothing in these CSCE declarations which specifically refers to equality for lesbians and gay men, it could be argued that the commitments to human rights 'for all' and 'without discrimination' are comprehensive and inclusive. With this liberal interpretation, these CSCE declarations implicitly oblige the signatory states to ensure equal treatment for lesbian and gay people in their laws and government policies.

The potential for the CSCE to be used as an instrument for the promotion of lesbian and gay equality throughout Europe was recognized by the Austrian homosexual rights organization Hosi Wien in 1986. In the run-up to the CSCE conference that year in Vienna, it lobbied the national delegations of every signatory state, urging them to raise the issue of lesbian and gay human rights.

Since then, there have been few attempts by the lesbian and gay movements to use the Helsinki Final Act and other CSCE agreements as a mechanism for the Europe-wide advancement of homosexual equality. This is unfortunate because the extension of the CSCE declarations to include human rights for homosexuals would be of great significance, particularly to the lesbian and gay communities in the more sexually-repressive East European countries — Albania, Bulgaria, Romania and the republics of the former Soviet Union — all of which are parties to the Helsinki Agreement and subsequent CSCE declarations. These countries are not members of the Council of Europe and are therefore not bound by any obligations under the European Convention on Human Rights. Their own national laws are very weak with regard to the protection of human rights in general and the rights of lesbians and gay men in particular. The CSCE agreements are thus the only definitive human rights commitments which their governments have signed and which lesbians and gay men in these countries can insist their governments honour. They are the only legal basis, however tenuous and contentious, that homosexuals have for pressuring their governments to legislate for lesbian and gay equality.

Government-level co-operation through the CSCE process has prompted the development of a parallel 'citizens movement from below'. The Helsinki Citizen's Assembly (HCA) seeks to unite social movements across Europe with the aim of pressuring governments to fulfil their CSCE pledges to human rights, disarmament and environmental protection. At its inaugural conference in Prague in October 1990, the HCA's Human Rights Commission urged all European governments to 'ensure full legal and social equality for lesbians and gay men', and called on the CSCE to enact amendments to the Helsinki Agreement 'outlawing discrimination and incitement to hatred on the grounds of a person's homosexuality'.[1]

The possibility that the CSCE might eventually become a more substantive framework for European co-operation was first proposed in 1989 by the West German Foreign Minister, Hans Dietrich Genscher, and by his Soviet counterpart Eduard Shevardnadze. They suggested that the CSCE could form the foundation of a new Europe-wide inter-governmental

institution. President Mitterrand went even further by proposing that the CSCE become a 'grand confederation' of European
states. A similar idea was put forward in 1991 by the US Secretary
of State, James Baker, who argued that the CSCE should evolve
into a 'Euro-Atlantic democratic community from Vancouver to
Vladivostok'. Some people in Eastern Europe, such as President
Havel of Czechoslovakia, also take the view that the CSCE is an
appropriate framework for future common European action
because it alone includes all the nations of the continent. It's an
opinion shared by many Green and Left parties in the West who
resent the West European exclusivity of the European Community (EC). Herman Verbeek, who is the only openly gay Member
of the European Parliament, argues for a CSCE-based European
federation: 'The name of the European Community is a fraud.
It only represents the western half of Europe. None of the East
European nations are part of the EC and the West seems
reluctant to let them join'. He also sees the CSCE as a potential
means to challenge the violation of lesbian and gay human rights
in countries like Bulgaria and Romania: 'There is a great need
for solidarity with our homosexual brothers and sisters in these
countries...I believe that a European Parliament, based on the
CSCE Helsinki institutions, could provide a useful forum to
promote lesbian and gay rights throughout every country in the
continent'.[2]

1   *Capital Gay*, 26 October 1990.
2   *Rouge*, Issue 3, summer 1990.

THE IMPLICATIONS OF
EUROPEAN INTEGRATION

The EC as the Focus for a United Europe

The growing impetus towards closer European co-operation is being fuelled by the East-West *rapprochement* following the demise of the Cold War, and by the recognition that all the European countries face common problems which can only be resolved by joint action. These shared concerns have led to demands all over Europe for agreements to cutback military expenditure, clean up toxic waste, avert food shortages in the former USSR, stop the depletion of the ozone layer, aid the ailing East European economies, and resolve ethnic and nation-alistic tensions in the disunited republics of what was previously Yugoslavia and the Soviet Union.

The realization that so many problems transcend national borders and are beyond the capability of individual govern-ments to put right, has greatly strengthened the case for a united Europe. Lesbian and gay demands for the eradication of dis-crimination from all European countries neatly coincide with this trend to closer integration and common action. It's a trend that we can exploit to our advantage. If there is going to be a united Europe, we can justifiably insist that it upholds equal rights for homosexuals throughout all its member states.

So far as the institutional framework of a united Europe is concerned, the most likely basis is the opening up of the European Community (EC) to a wider membership of nations. The EC is the only European institution which has the political and economic clout, and the decision-making structures, to implement common policies. Agreement to open EC member-ship to all the nations of Europe would therefore provide the most effective framework for joint action in a united Europe.

It has, however, been argued by those who are critical of the current West European exclusivity of the EC, that the merger of the Council of Europe and the Conference on Security and Co-operation in Europe (CSCE) might be a preferable mechanism for European integration, since most countries are already members. The biggest drawbacks to this idea are the limited agendas and powers of these two institutions. Both have little concern for social and economic matters.' Neither formulates day-to-day policy, and neither has legislative powers which are directly enforceable in the member states. For the Council of Europe and the CSCE to become the focus of a united Europe would require them to undergo a massive transformation.

By comparison, the EC has already laid the foundations of a European union, and is likely to evolve into a 30-plus grouping of nations by the year 2000. To date, new applications for membership have been submitted by Austria, Cyprus, Malta, Turkey and Sweden. Additional applications are expected soon from Finland, Iceland, Norway and Switzerland. In the meantime, formal associate membership of the EC is being sought by Bulgaria, Czechoslovakia, Hungary, Poland and Romania. EC co-operation agreements are being drawn up with Albania, Estonia, Latvia, Lithuania, and some of the independent republics which were formerly part of Yugoslavia and the Soviet Union. In October 1991, as a prelude to eventual full membership of the EC, the seven-nation European Free Trade Association agreed to join with the EC to create a European Economic Area; thereby incorporating the EFTA countries within the EC's Single European Market.

With so many countries aspiring to EC membership, it seems almost certain that the EC will become the primary focus for the creation of a united Europe. It therefore makes sence for the EC to also be the main target of Europe-wide campaigns for lesbian and gay rights. It's the institutional framework through which legislation for common policies for homosexual equality is likely to be most effective.

1992 — A Market or a Community?

The European Community (EC) was originally established in 1957 as the 'European Economic Community'. Despite some broadening of its concerns since then, it still has an overwhelmingly economic agenda. The current plans for the creation of a Single European Market are primarily concerned with the economic integration of the member states. The main aim is to break down the national barriers to production and trade within the EC in order to establish a 'common market' in capital, labour, goods and services. To achieve this, the EC is harmonizing product standards, technical and financial regulations, business laws and occupational qualifications. The key EC buzzwords are economic ones: Exchange Rate Mechanism, European Central Bank, Economic and Monetary Union and Single Currency. The intention is to establish an economic and trading bloc to compete with Japan and the United States.

'The EC is not really a community. It's just a market. It's only interested in business transactions, industrial production and economic growth...The creation of the Single European Market in 1992 is going to be very good for big business, but very bad for ordinary people', according to Herman Verbeek, MEP.[1]

To counter-balance this big business agenda, the Green and Left parties in the European Parliament, with the backing of many Liberals and Christian Democrats, won support for the idea of a 'Social Charter' to accompany the economic integration of 1992. They argued that a Social Charter was necessary to remedy the adverse effects of the Single European Market on the poorer peoples and regions of the EC. This demand was endorsed by progressive business sectors who feared that the Single European Market might give unfair cost-of-production advantages to member states and employers who paid low wages and provided low-standard working conditions. German-based manufacturers, for example, feared being undercut by rival companies using cheap labour in countries such as Portugal and Greece. Accordingly, the Social Charter, agreed by the Council of Ministers in December 1989, included commitments to common policies on fair wages and unemployment benefits, vocational training, equal treatment for women, industrial democracy, health and safety, and protection for young, elderly and disabled persons.

There is a strong argument that the lesbian and gay movements should adopt a similar strategy. EC integration is, to date, still largely an economic project. We must seek to make it a human rights project too. Taking advantage of the moves towards economic harmonization, and the impetus of the Social Charter, the lesbian and gay communities should demand a parallel 'human rights harmonization', including the adoption of common policies for lesbian and gay equality throughout the EC, based on the laws prevailing in the most progressive member states, Denmark and the Netherlands. If this upward harmonization, based on the most progressive practice, were to be achieved, it would result in a massive extension of equality for homosexuals in Britain and Ireland (the two most backward EC countries with regard to lesbian and gay rights).

Understandably, lesbian and gay campaigners in countries like Denmark, which have secured a high level of legal equality, are anxious that harmonization could lead to a levelling-down of civil rights; thereby eroding their hard-won gains of the last two decades. That's a danger we must guard against. However, it would be a tragedy if nationalist self-interest was allowed to override lesbian and gay solidarity across Europe. Surely our vision of lesbian and gay equality as a universal human right requires the strong and successful lesbian and gay movements to help those that are weaker and less influential.

A human rights harmonization which includes homosexual equality is still somewhat problematic. Because the EC was primarily set up as an economic institution, its legal mandate for action is largely restricted to economic policies. This means that the most likely gains the lesbian and gay communities can expect to win, under the existing economic-biased EC Treaties, is legislation to outlaw discrimination in employment. This could be enacted under the on-going Action Programme for the implementation of the Social Charter (which is already pledged to tackle discrimination against women, the disabled, and young and elderly people).

A wider EC social agenda, including an explicit human rights commitment, could emerge in the not too distant future with the proposed further revision of the EC Treaties. This might, eventually enable the EC to harmonize the laws of the member states to eradicate homophobic discrimination in non-economic spheres such as criminal law.

Herman Verbeek, MEP, is optimistic: 'I think the domination of the EC by big business...will eventually lead to a backlash against the EC's harsh materialism. When the demands for more humane EC policies explode, the lesbian and gay community must be ready to step forward with its own social and human rights agenda'.[2]

1   *Capital Gay*, 27 April 1990.
2   Ibid.

An Emerging European Super-State

Developments within the European Community (EC) point to the creation of an embryonic European super-state. Over the last decade, there has been a massive transfer of decision-making powers from the national governments of the 12 member countries to the European Commission and the Council of Ministers. Already, about 40 per cent of our legislation originates from Brussels. According to the President of the Commission, Jacques Delors, by the late 1990s up to 80 per cent of the laws affecting our lives will be decided at the European level.

The moves towards political union, with the ultimate goal of a federal Europe, will accelerate and formalize the establishment of a unified European state over the next decade. As this happens, the EC will replace national governments as the dominant institution of state power. This growth in the political authority of the EC is not something the lesbian and gay communities can afford to ignore. With legislative decision-making shifting to the EC in the wake of closer European integration, campaigns for lesbian and gay equality will also need to be increasingly directed at the EC institutions.

The limitations of this approach have been apparent following several votes in the European Parliament which have backed homosexual equality. The Dutch lesbian activist Willemien Ruygrok recalls: 'We got the Buron Report (which called for protection against homophobic discrimination in the workplace) carried by a big majority in the European Parliament. However...it was ignored by the Commission. This shows the lack of real democracy in the EC. The institutional structures are not accountable and therefore progressive decisions by the European Parliament can always be blocked by the Commission and the Council of Ministers'.[1]

This lack of democratic input and control is the crux of the problem. The emerging European state lacks even the basic rudiments of parliamentary democracy. All key decisions are taken by the unelected Council of Ministers, which are appointed by the national governments and are accountable to them alone. The Council meets in secret and issues no minutes of its proceedings. Many of its most important decisions require unanimous voting. A single reactionary member state can thus veto the adoption of progressive policies agreed by the other eleven. In contrast, the democratically elected and publicly accountable European Parliament is virtually powerless. It's limited delaying and amending powers can always be overridden by the Council of Ministers. Even more alarmingly, some recent EC policies — notably the Trevi and Schengen recommendations on terrorism, crime, immigration and refugees — have been agreed in top secret meetings outside the official EC decision-making framework.

The dearth of democracy and accountability in the EC has given rise to fears that it could develop into a centralized, secretive and authoritarian super-power.

Herman Verbeek, MEP of the Green Left in the Netherlands, sees the EC as a state without democratic legitimacy: 'How can you call it democratic when the European Commission and the Council of Ministers have no direct electoral mandate and take their decisions behind closed doors? The European Parliament is not a true parliament because it has no legislative powers. It's just a talking shop to give the EC a democratic facade'.[2]

This democratic deficit is a major obstacle to securing EC action against homophobia. The decision-making structures are not accessible to public scrutiny and popular pressure. This makes democratization of the evolving European state an important issue for the homosexual rights movement.

1   *The Pink Paper*, 12 May 1990.
2   *Capital Gay*, 27 April 1990.

The Need for a Euro-Strategy

'It is obvious that European unification is moving ahead fast', according to Nigel Warner of the International Lesbian and Gay Association. 'Unless lesbian and gay activists get in on the ground floor, we will find it difficult to influence this process. The longer we leave it, the harder it will become'.[1]

Fighting tomorrow's battles on yesterday's battlefields is pointless and demoralizing. With legislative authority shifting from the national to European level, the campaign for lesbian and gay equality has to shift in that direction too. As the European Community (EC) develops into a major centre of political power, the lesbian and gay communities will have to increasingly target their lobbying efforts at EC institutions. To do this effectively requires a well thought out strategy. In other words, a plan of action to transform EC policy in favour of lesbian and gay equality; thereby turning the EC into a positive asset for the advancement of homosexual rights throughout the continent.

There are four main ways of achieving this. Collectively, they add up to a coherent Euro-strategy involving:

- A liberal interpretation of the existing EC Treaties, whereby the general commitment of the Treaties to 'equality' and 'human rights' becomes accepted as a legal basis for EC action against homophobia.
- The revision of the EC Treaties to include an explicit pledge of lesbian and gay equality and to allow legislative decisions by a majority vote of the European Parliament.
- A new EC equality agenda, setting out concrete policies for lesbian and gay rights.

- The co-ordination of a Europe-wide campaign for homo-sexual equality, based on simultaneous lobbying in all the EC member states.

What's significant about this Euro-strategy is that it is proactive and assertive, rather than reactive and defensive. It goes on the political offensive, setting out a clear and credible plan of action for the advancement, at the EC level, of our demands for equality. Such a strategy is both necessary and feasible. In the opinion of the Dutch lesbian activist Willemien Ruygrok: 'I think this uplifting of laws to a higher level of equality for homosexuals throughout the EC is quite possible. It's certainly worth aiming for. I really want to see a common EC policy on lesbian and gay rights and I believe I will see it. By the year 2000, many more decisions will be taken at the EC level and I hope laws to guarantee lesbian and gay equality will be among them'.[2]

1   *The Pink Paper*, 21 April 1990.
2   *The Pink Paper*, 12 May 1990.

A EUROPEAN AGENDA FOR HOMOSEXUAL EQUALITY

Reinterpreting the Treaties of the EC

One of the main obstacles to European Community (EC) action in support of lesbian and gay equality is the illiberal way the Commission chooses to interpret the EC Treaties. It claims it is powerless to act because the EC Treaties contain no explicit commitment to homosexual rights. According to the Commission, the absence of a specific legal mandate under its Treaties means the EC has no competence to legislate against homophobic discrimination.

The narrow remit of the Treaties, particularly their lack of a detailed civil and human rights agenda, does make the legal case for EC action in support of lesbian and gay equality more difficult to argue. However, even within the limitations of the existing EC Treaties, it is possible to demonstrate how they could be liberally interpreted to legally legitimate anti-discrimination initiatives to protect homosexual people.

While it's true there is nothing concrete in the EC Treaties concerning lesbian and gay equality, there are numerous statements of general principles and objectives which could be construed as implicitly empowering the EC to protect the rights of homosexuals. Generous interpretations of the Treaties have been used in the past to justify EC initiatives on many other issues such as South Africa, data protection, racism, drug-trafficking, AIDS, and the Middle-East — none of which are explicitly referred to in the Treaties.

Human Rights & Harmonization

A liberal interpretation could argue that the EC has a legal competence and obligation to ensure equality and non-discrimination in general, and that this implicitly includes equality and non-discrimination for lesbians and gay men. The Preamble to the Treaty Establishing the European Economic Community in 1957 does, after all, contain comprehensive commitments to the promotion of 'human rights', 'liberty', 'freedom', 'equality', 'fundamental rights' and 'common policies'. It also includes pledges to achieve 'economic and social progress', 'common action to eliminate the barriers which divide Europe', and the 'constant improvement of the living and working conditions' of the people. These commitments constitute a plausible legal basis on which the EC could take initiatives to extend equal rights and non-discrimination to lesbians and gay men throughout the member states by means of the adoption of uniform policies. Indeed, the EC's failure to do so might arguably be a denial of these principles and thereby a failure to fulfil its legal obligations under its Treaties.

The EC also has sweeping powers under Article 235. In cases where the 'Treaty has not provided the necessary powers', this Article allows it to 'take the appropriate measures' necessary to attain 'the objectives of the Community'. Article 235 thus gives the EC wide interpretive powers and authorizes it to adopt policies on issues not specifically covered in the Treaties. Given that 'human rights', 'liberty', 'freedom' and 'equality' are stated as Treaty objectives, Article 235 does empower the EC to pursue these goals in the broadest sense. It could therefore be reasonably construed as giving the EC a *de facto* legal mandate to take action in pursuit of human rights, liberty, freedom and equality for lesbians and gay men.

So far as other EC Treaty obligations are concerned, the Preamble of the Single European Act specifies that one of the EC's aims is to 'improve the economic and social situation by extending common policies and pursuing new objectives'. This all-embracing remit could also be interpreted as providing a legal basis for EC action to ensure uniform equality laws for lesbians and gay men throughout the member states. By enacting legislation to provide EC-wide protection for the rights of homosexuals, the EC could be said to be 'extending common policies and pursuing new objectives' to 'improve the economic and social situation' of lesbians and gay men.

There are, furthermore, a number of specific Articles in the

Treaty Establishing the European Economic Community, and in the various amendments of the 1986 Single European Act, which could be said to give the EC an implicit legal competence to undertake measures to ensure equal and non-discriminatory treatment for lesbian and gay people in all the Community countries. The wide variations in the national laws of the 12 member states concerning the rights of homosexuals could, for example, be viewed as violating the Treaty commitments to 'harmonious development' (Article 2), 'closer relations between the States' (Article 2), 'approximation of the laws' (Article 3), 'establishment or functioning of the common market' (Article 100), 'improved working conditions and...their harmonization' (Article 117), 'harmonization of social systems' (Article 117), and 'close co-operation' in 'employment, labour law and work-ing conditions' (Article 118).

Freedom of Movement & Free Competition

The contradictory levels of legal repression and legal protection for lesbians and gay men in the different EC countries might be interpreted as being in contravention of the Treaty Articles which set out the EC's commitments to 'the abolition...of obstacles to the freedom of movement of persons' (Article 3), 'ensuring that competition in the common market is not dis-torted' (Article 3), 'freedom of movement for workers' (Article 48), 'abolition of any discrimination...as regards [to]...conditions of work and employment' (Article 48), 'abolishing those admin-istrative procedures and practices...the maintenance of which would form an obstacle to the liberalization of the movement of workers' (Article 49), 'the approximation of such provisions laid down by law...as directly affect the establishment of functioning of the common market' (Article 100), 'measures for the approxi-mation of the provisions...which have as their object the estab-lishment and functioning of the internal market' (Article 100a) and, in cases where differences in law are distorting competition in the common market, the taking of action 'eliminating the distortion in question' (Article 101).

It's arguable that there can be no genuine freedom of move-ment, and no absence of distorted competition, when fear of discrimination may discourage lesbian and gay people from freely moving around the EC because they face, in certain EC countries (especially Ireland and the UK), officially-sanctioned discrimination in employment and criminal law on the grounds of their sexuality.

Contrarily, some EC countries have employment advantages for homosexuals over other EC states because they have better legal rights for lesbians and gay men, such as laws prohibiting discrimination on the basis of sexual orientation (Denmark, France and the Netherlands). This could also be said to distort competition and impede the free movement of workers. Homosexual employees in countries where they are guaranteed legal protection against discrimination may be loathe to relocate in other EC member states where no such protection exists because they would thereby be vulnerable to discrimination. Furthermore, lesbian and gay employees in EC countries without legal protection against anti-homosexual discrimination may be encouraged to move to those member states which offer such protection. Either way, it would distort free competition in the labour market and put employers in EC countries with no anti-discrimination protection for lesbians and gay men at a disadvantage because they may not be able to retain or attract high-calibre employees who happen to be homosexual.

The following examples illustrate how the different laws pertaining to the rights homosexuals in the different EC countries may militate against genuine freedom of movement:

- Availing herself of the new mobility of labour in the Single European Market, a French lesbian might take up seasonal work in Germany. While there, she could face harassment from her employer if he discovers her sexuality. However, unlike in France, where there is comprehensive legal protection against discrimination on the grounds of sexual orientation, in Germany she will have no legal recourse to stop the harassment or to secure compensation.
- An American company might decide to locate its European headquarters in the United Kingdom. Staff from various EC countries would probably be seconded to the new headquarters. While in the UK, those personnel who are lesbian or gay would be rendered vulnerable to

discrimination and prosecution because of their sexuality in the following ways:

(a) They would have no legal protection against anti-homosexual discrimination in the workplace, including unfair dismissal or harassment by fellow employees, or against discrimination in the provision of public and private services such as housing.

(b) The male personnel could be liable to prosecution under the criminal law if they have sex with other men, unless both are aged 21 or over and their sexual acts occur in a private dwelling behind locked doors and windows, with no other person present in any part of the house.

(c) The gay male personnel (and the lesbian personnel in some circumstances) may also be liable to prosecution for consensual non-genital contacts (such as kissing, caressing, cruising, and exchanging telephone numbers in a public place) under the laws covering public order and morality, soliciting, importuning, procuring and indecency.

The Duty to Actively Promote Equality

The EC has more than a legal competence to act in support of lesbian and gay equality. It also has a legal responsibility to actively ensure compliance with the general objectives and specific provisions of its Treaties. These Treaties explicitly stipulate that the EC is authorized and required to 'promote' (i.e. encourage, facilitate and enact) measures for 'democracy... fundamental rights...freedom, equality and social justice' (Preamble of the Single European Act), 'harmonious development' (Article 2), 'closer relations between the States' (Article 2), 'improved working conditions' (Article 117), 'harmonization of social systems' (Article 117), 'approximation of provisions laid down by law, regulation or administrative action' (Article 117), and 'close co-operation between Member States in the social field' (Article 118).

This Treaty obligation to actively 'promote' equality and human rights is recognized by the Commission. In its booklet, *The European Community and Human Rights*, the Commission states that 'in the exercise of its powers it promotes those rights'.[1] This implies that the Commission has both a legal authority and an active commitment to the promotion of human rights objectives. Such an admission makes it difficult for the Commission to claim that action in pursuit of the human rights of lesbians and gay men falls outside its legal competence, and that it has no Treaty authority to proactively challenge homophobia.

Precedents for Liberal Interpretations

Generous interpretations of the EC Treaties, which would allow the enactment of policies to tackle anti-homosexual discrimination in employment, have already been made by the Legal Affairs Committee of the European Parliament. Meeting on 25 and 26 January 1984, it agreed:

'The Legal Affairs Committee takes the view that the objective of social progress laid down in the Treaty could justify Community action to ensure that homosexuals are not discriminated against in employment and that Article 117 (if necessary along with Article 235) is a valid legal basis for Community action to achieve this end'.[2]

The potential for a liberal interpretation of the EC Treaties is also illustrated by the Community Charter of the Fundamental Social Rights of Workers (the Social Charter). There is nothing in the EC Treaties about the rights of children and adolescents or elderly and disabled persons. Yet this has not stopped the Commission and the Council from including these categories of people within the Social Charter. Indeed, the Action Programme for the implementation of the Social Charter sets out concrete proposals for the elimination of discrimination against these disadvantaged sectors of the Community.[3] It could be plausibly argued that the legal basis for EC action to protect the young, elderly and disabled could also be used to incorporate lesbians and gay men within the Social Charter and the Action Programme.

The exclusion of homosexual people from the Social Charter is all the more indefensible given that the Preamble of the Charter states:

'Whereas in order to ensure equal treatment, it is important to combat every form of discrimination, including discrimination on the grounds of sex, colour, race, opinions and beliefs, and whereas, in a spirit of solidarity, it is important to combat social exclusion'.[4]

The Social Charter thus contains a categoric commitment to 'ensure equal treatment' and to 'combat social exclusion'. It also embodies an unambiguous pledge to tackle 'every form of discrimination'. Since homosexuals are a social grouping which undoubtedly suffers discrimination, this necessarily suggests an obligation to combat discrimination against lesbians and gay men. Regretfully, however, despite this all-embracing promise of non-discrimination, neither the Social Charter nor its Action Programme include any specific mention of the rights of homosexuals or any policy proposals in support of lesbian and gay equality.

Aids is a concrete example of the way the Commission and the Council of Ministers have pursued a liberal interpretation of the EC Treaties. Though none of the Treaties mention a word about Aids, a resolution 'On the Fight Against Aids' was agreed by the Council on 22 December 1989. Section III, 'The Fight Against Discrimination', states:

1. Any discrimination against persons with Aids or HIV-positive persons constitutes a violation of human rights and prejudices an effective prevention policy because of its effects of exclusion and ostracism.
2. The free movement of persons, goods and services in the Community and equal treatment as laid down in the Treaties are, and must continue to be, guaranteed.
3. The greatest possible vigilance must therefore be exercised in order to combat all forms of discrimination, particularly in recruitment, at the workplace, at school and as regards accommodation and sickness insurance.
4. With regard, more particularly, to accommodation and private insurance, solutions should be found which reconcile economic interests with the principle of non-discrimination.[5]

This resolution is an acknowledgement by the EC: (a) that it has legal authority and powers to undertake initiatives on issues not specifically covered by the EC Treaties; (b) that its anti-discrimination mandate can effectively include any issue of discrimination it chooses to act upon; (c) that the principle of the free movement of people within the Community involves more than merely the free movement of labour and economic mobility; (d) that the commitment to 'equal treatment' in the Treaties is not restricted to equal treatment on the grounds of nationality and sex; and (e) that the EC's anti-discrimination initiatives can involve more than economic and workplace matters, including rights in housing, education and insurance.

Until such time as the EC Treaties are revised to include a specific commitment to non-discrimination on the grounds of sexual orientation, further EC action in support of lesbian and gay equality will be largely dependent on winning the arguments about legal competence and securing a liberal interpretation of the Treaties.

1   *The European File Series*, European Commission, Luxemburg, April 1989, 5/89, p. 6.
2   *European Parliament Working Documents*, 1983-84, Document 1-1358/83, PE 87.477/fin., p. 30.
3   Com (89) 568 Final, European Commission, Brussels, 29 November 1989, p. 50-54.
4   *Community Charter of the Fundamental Social Rights of Workers*, European Commission, Luxemburg, 1990, p. 10.
5   *Official Journal of the European Communities*, No. C 10, 16. 1. 1990, p. 4.

Reforming the European Community

While securing a liberal interpretation of the existing EC Treaties is an immediate objective, the ultimate goal is a major overhaul of those Treaties. Already there have been strong demands for reform, with the European Parliament voting overwhelmingly in 1990 in favour of proposals by the British Labour MEP David Martin. The Martin Report called for the expansion of the EC's remit into the spheres of social policy and human rights; for the European Parliament to have co-equal decision-making powers with the Council of Ministers; and for the extension of majority voting to a wider range of issues. Each of these changes would greatly strengthen the likelihood of EC action in support of homosexual equality. This suggests that the struggle for lesbian and gay rights in the EC is closely bound up with the struggle for the reform of EC institutions.

At the EC Maastricht summit in December 1991, the presidents and prime ministers of the member states took the first hesitant steps in the direction of EC reform. They agreed that more decisions in the Council of Ministers should be by majority vote, rather than by unanimity. They also agreed that the European Parliament should be granted the power of veto over Council of Ministers' legislation on a small number of issues (but still no authority to initiate legislation). The reforms at Maastricht were thus very modest. They did little to democratize the EC or to strengthen its human rights commitment.

There are, however, four much more radical reforms which, if enacted, would very significantly increase the possibility of EC action against homophobia.

Human Rights Agenda

The absence in the EC Treaties of any specific and detailed Articles concerning human rights makes it much easier for the EC to evade tackling anti-gay discrimination. One way of remedying this is by revising the Treaties to include an explicit commitment to the active promotion of equality for everyone and the active eradication of all forms of discrimination, including on the grounds of sexuality. This would thereby ensure that the EC had an unambiguous legal mandate, and an unavoidable legal obligation, to rectify the abrogation of lesbian and gay human rights. With such a change in the Treaties, the EC could no longer plead that action on homosexual equality was outside its legal competence. Discriminatory policies which violated the rights of lesbians and gay men could therefore be directly challenged and overturned in the European Court of Justice — the EC's *de facto* supreme court. It is the final arbiter of EC law, with the power to issue judgements which are legally binding on the EC and its member states. This reform would give lesbians and gay men substantive new powers of redress against homophobia in EC and national government policy; covering not only explicit acts of direct discrimination, but also implicit and indirect discrimination by the omission of protection for homosexual people from official policies.

Power to the Parliament

With no effective mechanism for the democratic control and public accountability of EC decision-making, campaigns for lesbian and gay equality always come up against institutional obstacles when seeking changes in policy. The real centre of power in the EC, the Council of Ministers, is secretive and unelected. This makes attempts to influence its decisions very difficult. There are therefore strong democratic arguments in favour of transferring the EC's prime legislative authority from the Council of Ministers to the European Parliament. The emerging EC super-state is, after all, almost totally bereft of even the most basic elements of parliamentary democracy. Since the parliament is the only truly democratic and representative EC institution, surely it ought to be the ultimate policy-making body, with the Council of Ministers having limited delaying and amending powers over parliamentary legislation. This reform would open up EC decision-making to improved scrutiny and accountability. The greater accessibility to the sources of legislative power, together with the more liberal-minded attitudes of MEPs, would much enhance effective lobbying on issues of concern to the lesbian and gay communities. Our chance of getting positive policies would correspondingly increase.

Majority Voting

At present, many important decisions in the Council of Ministers are required, under the EC Treaties, to be agreed by a unanimous vote. A policy accepted by eleven member states can thus be vetoed by the twelfth. This severely limits the possibility of the EC implementing progressive policies on lesbian and gay issues: if a homosexual equality initiative was proposed by the Dutch or Danish governments, it could always be blocked by the UK or Ireland. This obstacle to legislation against homophobia could, however, be overcome if there was a switch to majority voting. Most EC countries now have equal ages of consent and non-discriminatory penal codes. Some have laws which protect lesbians and gay men against discrimination and prohibit incitement to hatred against homosexuals. The extension of majority voting to all EC policy-making is therefore likely to enhance the probability of lesbian and gay rights legislation being enacted.

Wider Membership

The opening up of the EC to a wider membership of nations may well extend the number of pro-gay member states and thereby increase the pressure for EC action in support of homosexual equality. Among the countries likely to join the EC in the next few years are Czechoslovakia, Norway, Sweden and Switzerland. These countries have progressive laws on lesbian and gay rights and their membership of the EC would add further votes in the European Parliament and the Council of Ministers in support of equality. There are, however, other prospective EC member states which have a bad record on homosexual rights — Austria, Cyprus, Hungary and Turkey. If they joined the EC, it could have the positive effect of encouraging them to repeal their homophobic laws to bring their criminal codes into line with the EC majority. However, if they persisted with their anti-gay policies, it might have the negative effect of cancelling out the increase in pro-gay opinion brought about by the membership of liberal-minded countries like Norway and Sweden. On balance, given that the historical trend is shifting in favour of homosexual equality, a wider EC membership is likely to encourage the harmonization of gay-related legislation based on best practice rather than worst.

Equality in the European Community

As the EC institutions evolve into a fully-fledged European state, the question of citizen's rights is becoming ever more important. Already, the EC has enormous, and growing, influence over our lives. Yet the citizens of the member countries have no rights and freedoms guaranteed by EC law and no legal mechanisms for the direct redress of abuses of EC power. In short, we are now part of an embryonic European state where the rights of citizens are neither recognized nor protected. This has potentially grave dangers for civil liberties.

Concomitantly, the explosion of EC policy directives is sometimes reinforcing and even exacerbating social disparities and iniquities. While the EC is attempting to address some aspects of disadvantage and discrimination in the economic sphere, general issues of equality are largely being ignored. This is having a particularly adverse effect on marginalized social groups who, currently, look set to gain very little from European integration.

The need for specific EC constitutional and legislative guarantees concerning the civil rights of citizens, and the right of all citizens to equal treatment, is likely to assume even greater importance as the new European state extends its powers in the coming years. It is given an added urgency by the surge of Fascist and racist movements across much of Europe.

Already suffering a denial of basic human rights, lesbians and gay men have a strong interest in ensuring that EC officials and policies are subject to constitutional checks and balances, and to specific legal commitments and obligations, regarding equal treatment for all sectors of society. It's an interest we share with other disadvantaged social groups such as women, black people, migrant workers and the disabled.

This recognition points to the need for an all-inclusive equality agenda to ensure equal rights for everyone — as opposed to a separate and exclusive agenda for homosexual equality alone. A comprehensive approach of 'equal rights for all', which incorporates equality for lesbian and gay people within a broader equality agenda, is the tactic most likely to avoid the marginalization of our concerns and most likely to secure their integration into the mainstream of EC policies. It's also probably the best way to minimize the level of homophobic backlash. By arguing from the standpoint that every person has a right to equal treatment and protection against discrimination, it's much harder for our opponents to discredit us and much easier for us to win public acceptance for our demands. The 'all-in' approach to equality also has the advantage of helping to build mutually empowering alliances between lesbians and gay men and other people struggling against discrimination. This gives us a common interest in pooling our resources and working together around a joint agenda for our shared benefit; thereby optimizing our chances of success.

There are three key policies which, more than any others, would help to secure equality and non-discrimination within the EC: a Bill of Rights, an Anti-Discrimination Directive and an Equal Opportunities Executive. These three policies would collectively contribute to the creation of a democratic and egalitarian legal framework which upholds the human rights of all EC citizens and which constrains the otherwise uncontrolled power of the emergent European state. While they would not guarantee that the EC never again violates the rights of lesbian and gay people, these policies would make such violations much more difficult.

Bill of Rights

Nearly every modern democratic state has a constitution which enshrines inviolable rights and freedoms for its citizens. The fledgeling EC state does not.

For lesbians and gay men, the enactment of an EC Bill of Rights, with explicit guarantees of equality on the grounds of sexuality, would give significant new protection against discrimination (especially in repressive countries like Britain and

Ireland). It would do this by placing severe restraints on the power of the EC and national governments to legislate anti-gay policies, and also by providing mechanisms for the striking down by the courts of any such measures already enacted. An EC Bill of Rights would also help establish common minimum standards of equality binding on the current member countries and on any other countries applying for membership in the future. This would make the accession of homophobic states like Cyprus and Romania conditional on their repeal of anti-homosexual laws.

An EC Bill of Rights would need to include a comprehensive and explicit clause guaranteeing homosexual equality to avoid the danger of homophobic misinterpretation by the judiciary (as has happened to Bills of Rights in the United States and the Council of Europe); possibly along the following lines:

> 'Everyone shall be entitled, in all circumstances and without distinction, to full and equal rights under the law, to equality of opportunity, and to legal protection against discrimination on any grounds whatsoever, including sex, race, national or social origin, religion, language, political opinion or belief, age, sexual identity or orientation, disability or medical condition.'

Anti-Discrimination Directive

An EC Bill of Rights would be useful in enabling anti-gay legislation and court rulings to be challenged and overturned. However, legal and constitutional appeals take a long time (usually more than two years). They do not, therefore, offer a swift remedy for day-to-day discrimination against particular individuals — as in the case of a lesbian or gay employee who is dismissed because of their sexuality.

To enable such people to get faster and more effective personal redress, including restitution of their rights and compensation, requires a specific and concrete EC Anti-Discrimination Directive; similar to legislation that already exists in Denmark and France, and directly enforceable in all courts of law throughout the EC. This would give discriminated individuals direct legal powers to get injunctions and win damages from the perpetrators. The wording of such a Directive could be as follows:

> 'It shall be unlawful to discriminate against a person, or group of persons,
> (a) in any circumstances whatsoever — including laws and practice concerning employment, partnership, housing, sexual offences, education, health-care, censorship, political asylum, child custody, immigration, fostering and adoption, military service, donor insemination, government and judicial administration, and the provision of goods and services; and
> (b) on any grounds whatsoever — including sex,race, national or social origin, religion, language, political opinion or belief, age, sexual identity ororientation, disability, HIV status, or other medical condition.
> All persons suffering discrimination shall be entitled to legal redress, including the restitution of their rights and compensation. The perpetrators of acts of discrimination shall be liable to a maximum penalty of an equivalent of £50,000 fine and/or one year's imprisonment, plus the payment of compensation to the victims of their discrimination'.

Equal Opportunities Executive

There is little value in the EC having a Bill of Rights and an Anti-Discrimination Directive unless there is also an agency to ensure they work effectively. One way of doing this is through the creation of an EC Equal Opportunities Executive, attached to the European Commission, with the authority to monitor, promote and enforce equality of access and opportunity for everyone, including lesbians and gay men.

The Executive's role could include giving expert advice on the impact on equal rights of new EC legislation, and providing legal representation to those bringing court cases challenging discrimination. It could also have responsibility for scrutinizing the practices of all EC institutions and national government departments and, where necessary, issuing legally-binding recommendations to remedy discrimination.

As part of a long-term EC programme to eradicate inequality, the Equal Opportunities Executive's remit might extend to the setting of statutory EC-wide Equality Targets and Equality Codes of Practice, including the requirement for all major public and private institutions in the EC to compile annual Equality Audits and undertake Equality Impact Assessments before new policies are finalized.

Campaigning Across the European Community

Winning new EC policies for homosexual equality requires concerted and simultaneous campaigning directed at all aspects of EC influence and decision-making by the lesbian and gay movements in every member state. Thus far, however, campaigning has been undertaken by only a handful of organizations — mainly in the Netherlands, Belgium and the UK. It has failed to fully mobilize potential allies within the EC structures and has focused on lobbying the European Parliament and the European Commission to the neglect of other EC institutions and modes of pressure.

International Lesbian & Gay Association

The International Lesbian and Gay Association (ILGA) has a central co-ordinating role to play in the campaign for equality at the EC level. It's the organizational framework through which information and ideas can be most effectively exchanged between the movements in the different countries, and through which the lobbying of the EC can be best planned and executed.

ILGA was founded in 1978 with the aim of monitoring, publicizing, and campaigning against the oppression of homosexuals the world over. It's membership currently comprises 300 lesbian and gay organizations in 50 countries. Promoting international lesbian and gay solidarity, ILGA co-ordinates 'twinning' projects (including exchange visits and financial aid) between lesbian and gay movements in the West and those in Third World and East European countries, where poverty and dictatorship often exacerbate the difficulty of struggling for homosexual emancipation.

In recent years, ILGA has helped organize successful international campaigns to persuade the Council of Europe and the

European Parliament to agree resolutions condemning discrimination against lesbians and gay men, and to get Amnesty International to adopt people imprisoned for their homosexuality as 'prisoners of conscience'.

Committed to the principle that equality for lesbians and gay men is an issue of fundamental human rights, ILGA is currently seeking official consultative status with the Council of Europe and the United Nations to give it a direct input into the decision-making processes of these important international human rights institutions. Though ILGA's initial applications to the UN and the Council of Europe were rejected, in 1990 and 1991 respectively, it is continuing to lobby member states and plans to reapply for consultative status in the near future.

ILGA is also seeking the amendment of the European Convention on Human Rights (ECHR) and the United Nations Universal Declaration of Human Rights to include an explicit commitment to the principle of non-discrimination on the grounds of sexual orientation. In May 1990, at a fringe conference in Copenhagen which ran parallel with the official Conference on the Human Dimensions of the CSCE, ILGA launched its campaign for a new protocol to the ECHR. This protocol would explicitly guarantee legal equality for lesbians and gay men and would outlaw discrimination based on sexual orientation.

In recent years, ILGA has spearheaded the lobbying of the EC. It has met with the Social Affairs Commissioner, drawn up a report on the impact of the Single European Market on lesbians and gay men, secured a Code of Practice which recommends action against homophobic harassment in the workplace, and drafted questions and resolutions for the European Parliament. It's immediate aim is a legally-binding EC Directive outlawing employment discrimination against lesbians and gay men.

Lobbying Tactics

The EC includes a range of institutions with a diversity of powers and methods of influence, many of which have never been fully exploited by the lesbian and gay movement. In ascending order of political power they are:

Economic and Social Committee — It is made up of representatives of employers, trade unions and consumer groups. Under EC regulations, they have the right to be consulted on all economic and social issues before the Council of Ministers makes a final policy decision. Though the members of this Committee lack legislative power, their views do have influence. A recommendation from the Committee in support of homosexual equality would, for example, help reinforce the demands already being made by the European Parliament and lesbian and gay organizations. It's a means of pressure that could be pursued through the Trade Union Congress, which has comprehensive policies in support of lesbian and gay rights. The TUC is represented on the Economic and Social Committee through its EC equivalent, the European Trade Union Confederation (ETUC). Getting the ETUC to lobby for homosexual equality within the Committee would usefully add to the pressure for action which is being applied by other means on the European Commission and the Council of Ministers.

European Parliament — Members of the European Parliament (MEPs) have relatively little power. Nevertheless, their decisions do carry a growing moral weight which the Commission and the Council of Ministers are less likely to ignore in the future (the European Parliament's powers will probably be significantly increased in the next revision of the EC Treaties). Lobbying the European Parliament can take the form of targeting a local constituency MEP or all the MEPs on a particular parliamentary committee (the Civil Liberties and Internal Affairs, Legal & Citizen's Rights, Social & Employment, and Women's Rights committees tend to be of greatest relevance and sympathy to lesbian and gay concerns). It can also involve petitioning the European Parliament. All citizens of the EC member states have the right to submit petitions on any subject. Usually, they are appeals against EC legislation on the grounds that it violates the EC Treaties and has resulted in some form of unfair treatment. Thus, the basis for a lesbian and gay rights petition could be the Social Charter's failure to give homosexuals the same level of protection against discrimination as it pledges for women and for young, elderly and disabled persons. Petitions submitted to the European Parliament are considered by the Committee on

Petitions. It is empowered to organize formal parliamentary hearings and to propose resolutions for debate. It can also demand explanatory information and remedial action from the European Commission.

European Commission — It has the authority to initiate and implement EC legislation. This gives the Commission considerable power. The most effective way for lesbian and gay organizations to influence the Commission is by lobbying the Commissioners from their own country (the larger EC countries appoint two commissioners and the smaller nations one), or by making approaches to the Social Affairs Commissioner within whose remit most gay-related issues fall. There is also the option of using the Commission's formal complaints procedure. Complaints can be brought on the grounds that particular policies violate the EC Treaties. A complaint could thus be brought arguing that discrimination against homosexuals in the member states is an impediment to the free movement of people and is contrary to the pledges of respect for human rights — as set out in the EC Treaties which the Commission is legally bound to uphold. Failing a satisfactory ruling from the Commission, the complaint could be taken to the European Court of Justice. This is the EC's supreme judicial body. It has the power to compel EC institutions and member state governments to act in accordance with the EC Treaties. It can also quash EC legislation which it judges to be in violation of these treaties.

Council of Ministers — As the principle policy-making body in the EC, the Council of Ministers is the most important to influence. Consisting of the relevant government Ministers from each of the 12 member states, the Council's composition depends on the issue under discussion. If it's to do with employment, the Council will comprise the 12 Employment Ministers from the national governments. Lobbying the Council of Ministers to support homosexual equality initiatives therefore requires targeting the Ministers involved in decisions on subjects of concern to the lesbian and gay communities. Securing a common EC policy granting refugee status to non-EC citizens persecuted because of their homosexuality would, for example, involve targeting foreign ministers. The President of the Council of Ministers is a particularly significant target. The Presidency rotates between the member states, in alphabetical order, every six months. The President has a lot of power to prepare recommendations and to initiate new policies. Pressuring the Presidency when it is held by governments which are progressive on lesbian and gay rights is another valuable way of getting our issues taken up by the EC. (The governments of the Netherlands and Denmark are likely to be the most sympathetic.)

Co-ordination & Alliances

While ILGA has done much useful campaigning within the EC, its biggest weakness has been its inability to orchestrate simultaneous campaigns by all its affiliated groups — something which is of crucial importance to any strategy for lesbian and gay reforms at the EC level. 'There are considerable differences within ILGA concerning our EC strategy', according to Co-General Secretary Lisa Power. 'The Spanish are enthusiastic, whereas the Danish are more reluctant and suspicious of the EC. This makes it difficult to co-ordinate a Europe-wide campaign'. As a result, ILGA's annual regional conference of member organizations in Europe is more a loose network than a centre for co-ordinated campaigning. This is clearly inadequate to meet the challenge of the 1990s, as the EC makes more and more decisions which affect our communities. What is urgently needed is the formalization of ILGA's existing European network into a Federation of EC Lesbian & Gay Organizations which can pool their resources and organize joint campaigns by all the lesbian and gay movements throughout all the member states. Our aim should be to bring pressure to bear on every EC institution from all sides, involving lesbian and gay groups in every corner of the EC: from Greece to Ireland and from Portugal to Denmark.

Building alliances with non-lesbian and gay political parties and social movements is also important. Since we are not a majority, we can never hope to win human rights solely by our own efforts. Support from outside the lesbian and gay community is essential.

In the European Parliament, the Left and Green parties have consistently advocated homosexual equality. All five resolutions in support of lesbian and gay rights have been sponsored by either Socialist or Communist MEPs. To extend this base of support to Liberals and Christian Democrats, we need a full-time Brussels-based EC liaison office to develop closer ties with sympathetic MEPs and with supportive officials working for the European Commission. Such an office could perform the functions of monitoring EC legislation, drafting parliamentary questions and resolutions, and proposing amendments to the policies of the European Commission and the Council of Ministers. It could also usefully co-ordinate a European network of pro-gay rights MPs in the national and regional parliaments of the member states who could be called upon, as the need arises, to lobby their government's representatives in the European Commission and the Council of Ministers.

There is also mutual advantage to be gained from co-operation with other EC-wide social movements campaigning around equality issues such as the rights of women and immigrants, and with pan-European forums like the Helsinki Citizen's Assembly and the mass campaigns against the rise of Fascism and racism. It is through collective solidarity, over-riding national boundaries and sectional interests, that we have our surest hope of eventually winning equality for the 32 million lesbian and gay citizens of the EC.

A GUIDE TO
LESBIAN & GAY RIGHTS
IN EUROPE

Summary of the Guide

Over recent decades, for the first time in human history, lesbian and gay people have gradually begun to win a semblance of legal equality with heterosexual men and women. This guide sets out the positive legislative reforms that have already improved the quality of life of lesbians and gay men in many European countries. It also points to the reforms that have still to be won to end legal discrimination against homosexual people.

The guide covers 32 European countries, East and West, with a combined population of 820 million people. Of these, an estimated 80 million Europeans are predominantly or exclusively lesbian or gay, and a further 120 million are estimated to be bisexual for all or part of their lives.

Almost every European country has, at some point in its history, decreed a total ban on homosexuality. In most cases, the ban applied solely to sex between men. Only seven countries have also had a complete prohibition on lesbianism — Austria, Bulgaria, Czechoslovakia, Finland, Hungary, Romania and Sweden.

The first European countries to decriminalize homosexual relations were France in 1791, Belgium and Luxemburg in 1792, the Netherlands in 1811 and Spain in 1822.

Today, the overwhelming majority of European countries have at least partially legalized same-sex relationships. Only seven countries still have a total ban on male homosexual acts — Cyprus, Estonia, Ireland, Latvia, Lithuania, Romania and the ex-Soviet Union (plus the former Yugoslav republics of Bosnia-Herzegovina, Macedonia and Serbia). In the sole case of Romania, the proscriptions against homosexuality also explicitly renders lesbianism illegal.

Ages of Consent

Seven countries have repealed the complete ban on homosexual contacts, but still enforce a discriminatory age of consent which is higher for homosexuals than for heterosexuals (on average it is 18 years for same-sex relationships compared with 15 years for sex between men and women) — Austria, Bulgaria, Finland, Hungary, Iceland, Luxemburg, and the United Kingdom (plus the ex-Yugoslav republic of Croatia and the western half of Germany). The UK has the highest age of consent for homosexuals anywhere in Europe: 21 years. The discriminatory ages of consent also apply to lesbians in three of these countries — Bulgaria, Finland and Hungary.

Sixteen countries have equal ages of consent for heterosexuals and lesbian and gay people, with the average age being 15 years — Albania, Belgium, Czechoslovakia, Denmark, France, Greece, Italy, Malta, Netherlands, Norway, Poland, Portugal, Spain, Sweden, Switzerland and Turkey (plus the ex-Yugoslav republics of Slovenia and Montenegro and the eastern half of Germany). Spain has the lowest common age of consent at 12 years. The Netherlands doesn't prosecute sex with 12-15 year olds unless there is a complaint. In Albania and Italy, the age of consent is 14 years for heterosexuals and homosexuals alike.

The legal codes of most countries do not specifically refer to lesbianism. In practice, the age of consent for sexual relations between women is usually deemed to be the same as that for heterosexual women.

Equality & Protection

So far as other legislation on homosexuality is concerned:

- Anti-discrimination protection for lesbians and gay men is enforced in five countries — Denmark, France, Netherlands, Norway and Sweden. The judicial interpretation of the constitution of the Netherlands, and specific laws in the other four countries, variously make it an offence to discriminate against lesbians and gay men in employment, the provision of goods and services, and access to public facilities. Similar comprehensive anti-discrimination legislation is currently being proposed to the Belgian and Dutch parliaments, and is also included in the draft constitution of the eastern German state of Brandenburg.

- Laws against public insults and incitement to hatred on the grounds of a person's sexual orientation exist in three countries — Denmark, Ireland and Norway. The introduction of comparable legislation is under consideration in Belgium and the Netherlands.
- Political asylum has been granted to lesbians and gay men, on the grounds that they were at risk of persecution in their home countries because of their sexuality, by six states — Austria, Denmark, Germany, Netherlands, Norway and Sweden (though asylum is granted at the government's discretion, on a case-by-case basis, and not as a statutory right).
- Lesbian and gay partnerships are officially recognized in two countries: Danish homosexual couples have the right to civil marriage at a registry office and enjoy all the legal rights of married heterosexuals, except for child adoption. Swedish lesbian and gay lovers who live together enjoy the same substantial legal rights as cohabiting heterosexual couples. Additionally, although not explicitly recognized in law, Dutch same-sex partners who confirm their relationship by legal contract are eligible for some of the rights granted to married heterosexual people. In Italy, there is a *de facto* legal recognition of homosexual couples at the level of municipal administration (though this recognition grants no legal rights to the partners concerned). France, Netherlands, Norway and Sweden are now looking at Danish-style civil marriage legislation that would allow lesbian and gay partners to register their relationship and enjoy legal status similar to married heterosexuals.
- Immigration and residence rights on the basis of a committed homosexual relationship are available, at the discretion of the authorities, to the foreign partners of lesbians and gay men in four countries — Denmark, Netherlands, Norway and Sweden.
- Membership in the armed forces is open to homosexuals in eleven countries — Austria, Belgium, Denmark, Germany,

Finland, France, Netherlands, Norway, Spain, Sweden and Switzerland — providing sexual relationships take place outside of barracks during off-duty hours. In the German armed forces, however, homosexuals are barred from officer rank.

Discrimination

Despite much progress in the last 30 years towards homosexual equality, in many European countries there is still widespread legal discrimination and personal prejudice against lesbians and gay men in employment, fostering and adoption, partnership, housing, sex education, political asylum, child custody, immigration, donor insemination, military service and sexual offences law.

- The promotion of homosexuality is banned in three countries — Austria, Finland and the United Kingdom. In addition, the Turkish government bought charges of 'spreading homosexual information' against lesbian and gay activists in 1989.
- The UK has more laws which explicitly, or in practice, discriminate against homosexuals than any other European nation, East or West. More gay and bisexual men are prosecuted in the UK for consenting homosexual behaviour than in any other country in Europe.
- The UK is the only European country to have introduced new anti-gay laws (Section 28) in the last decade. The enactment of this legislation goes against the liberalizing trend towards greater legal equality for homosexuals throughout the rest of the continent.
- There are only three places in Europe where anal intercourse is still punishable by life imprisonment — Ireland, Gibraltar and the Isle of Man. In all three cases, the anti-gay laws were originally introduced by the British during the period of colonial rule. In the cases of Gibraltar and the Isle of Man, Britain still has ultimate responsibility for their observance of international human rights agreements. So far, it has declined to intervene to ensure their compliance

with agreements such as the European Convention on Human Rights which has been interpreted as requiring states to decriminalize homosexuality.

- Denmark, Netherlands, Norway and Sweden are the most liberal countries in Europe with regard to recognizing and protecting the human rights of their lesbian and gay citizens. These countries provide concrete examples of the progressive and practical legislation that can be enacted to ensure homosexual equality.

Guide to Britain

Sexual Offences Laws

Lesbianism has never been an offence under British law. Occasionally, however, general laws are used to convict lesbian women for consensual sex. The most notorious recent case concerned 18-year-old Jennifer Saunders. She was charged with indecent assault after she allegedly posed as a boy to seduce two 17-year-old women. In September 1991, Doncaster Crown Court heard that Saunders had sex with one of the women six times a week throughout their five month affair, often using a strap-on plastic penis. The relationships were entirely consensual. However, both women claimed they did not know that Saunders was a woman and would have not consented to sex with her if they had been aware of her true female identity. Saunders protested that she had only dressed as a boy at the women's request, because they were embarrassed at having a lesbian relationship and didn't want their family and friends to find out. Sentencing Saunders to six years imprisonment, Judge Jonathon Crabtree said the women had been cruelly deceived and would have been 'better able to cope if they had been raped by a man'.[1]

Male homosexual relations were completely illegal in the UK until 1967. In that year, the Sexual Offences Act decriminalized gay sex in England and Wales between two consenting men in private aged 21 and over. The provisions of the 1967 Act were only extended to Scotland in 1980 and to Northern Ireland in 1982. They still do not apply to those serving in the armed forces and the merchant navy.

Despite the ostensible decriminalization of male homosexuality, there remain on the statute books wide-ranging laws against consenting gay relations. The four main homosexual-related offences are buggery (anal sex), indecency (gay sex other than buggery, such as mutual masturbation and fellatio), soliciting (cruising and propositioning men), and procuring (inviting, encouraging, and facilitating homosexual acts).

Consensual buggery and indecency between men are still crimes if they take place outside the privacy of a person's own home; if they involve men under the age of 21; and if they include the participation or presence of more than two people. Consensual soliciting and procuring were not even partially decriminalized by the 1967 Act. Cruising and aiding and abetting homosexual relations are therefore still crimes in all circumstances. The maximum penalties for these four gay offences are two years imprisonment if both men are over 21, or five years if one of the partners is aged 16-21. Equivalent heterosexual behaviour is either not a crime or is hardly ever prosecuted.

Britain's sexual offences laws thus continue to criminalize every form of consenting gay behaviour outside the strict legal exemption: between two consenting men aged 21 or over in private.

Under Section 1 of the 1967 Sexual Offences Act, the age of consent for gay relations remains at 21. For heterosexual men and women and lesbians it is 16 (except in Northern Ireland where it's 17). In 1989, 31 men aged 21 or over were gaoled for consenting behaviour with other men aged 16-21.[2] The longest sentences received ranged from three to four years. During the same year, 185 teenagers were convicted and 147 were cautioned for the predominantly — thought not exclusively — gay and consensual offences of buggery, soliciting, indecency and procuring.[3] Four of these teenagers were sentenced to youth custody for consenting indecency and soliciting, and ten were given custody for buggery 'with a boy under 16, or a woman or animal'.

Section 1 also stipulates that all sex between men continues to be totally illegal if more than two people participate or are present. This tight definition of privacy was used to justify a 2:00A.M. police raid on a private birthday party at the home of Martin Johnson in Acton, West London, in October 1982. On the suspicion that gay sex was taking place in the bedrooms, and the fact that more than two people were present in the house, the police arrested all 37 guests (though they later dropped the case).[4]

Many of the laws under which gay men are charged were never intended by parliament to be used to repress homosexuality. Police and judges have taken it upon themselves to interpret the law in the most homophobic way possible. Typical of this illiberal interpretation of the law is the use of Section 32 of the 1956 Sexual Offences Act against gay and bisexual men. It was originally introduced in 1898 to combat heterosexual men seeking female prostitutes. Under this legislation, 'it is an offence for a man persistently to solicit or importune in a public place for immoral purposes'. Despite decriminalization in 1967, homosexual behaviour is still deemed by the police and courts to be an 'immoral purpose'. This means it is unlawful for two consenting men to cruise or chat-up each other in a public place with a view to arranging sexual relations — even if they never have sex. Judges have interpreted soliciting and importuning as including any form of communication, ranging from verbal propositions and passing notes, to merely smiling and winking at another man. This results in the legal anomaly that it is a criminal offence for homosexuals to meet each other for the purpose of arranging sexual relations which are completely lawful.

The post-1967 'immoral' status of homosexuality was reinforced in 1973 when the House of Lords upheld the conviction of the publishers of *International Times* on charges of 'conspiracy to corrupt public morals' following the magazine's publication of gay contact advertisements.

The two other main discriminatory sexual offences are 'indecency between men' and 'procuring' homosexual acts. The laws against homosexual procuring make it a crime to invite, encourage, facilitate or aid and abet gay sex. According to Section 4 of the 1967 Sexual Offences Act it is an offence to procure a man to have anal sex with another man — even if he is willing and even if the act procured is perfectly legal in that it involves two consenting men aged 21 or over in private. Section 13 of the 1956 Sexual Offences Act criminalizes the procuring of an act of indecency between men. This offence overwhelmingly takes place with the cognizance and agreement of the participants. It can include things like propositioning a man to have homosexual intercourse in a non-private place such as a heathland;

encouraging or assisting more than two men to have group sex; and inviting a male teenager aged 16-21 to have homosexual relations. In 1991, a West Midlands man was prosecuted for procuring after the police accidentally discovered a private video that he had made of two male friends having sex in his house. Additionally, because the two friends were respectively aged 17 and 24, the older partner was charged with unlawful buggery.

'Indecency between men' is a crime under Section 13 of the 1956 Sexual Offences Act. It is a wholly consensual offence. Most convictions for indecency relate to sexual behaviour in parks and toilets. The men are usually arrested as a result of police surveillance and entrapment operations, as opposed to genuine complaints from members of the public who have witnessed explicit genital acts. Heterosexual lover's-lanes are never subject to similar operations, and men and women caught having sex in such locations are normally let off with a warning or a caution. For homosexuals it's different. In December 1988, a 37-year-old man was given a nine month suspended sentence for indecency. Arrested again, in July 1989 he was sentenced to 18 months gaol at Northampton Crown Court for merely 'fondling and kissing' a 17-year-old youth in a deserted church courtyard in the middle of the night.[5] More recently, in the summer of 1991, nearly 30 men were convicted of indecency in an obscure woodland in Epsom; many receiving fines of £1,000.

As well as bringing charges of indecency under the 1956 Act, the police are increasingly using the indecency clauses of local authority and public transport bye-laws to prosecute gay and bisexual men. This allows them to deny the defendants the right to trial by jury. Unlike those arrested on Section 13 indecency charges, gay men facing prosecution under bye-laws cannot choose trial by jury. They are tried by magistrates alone and they are less likely to be granted legal aid. As a result, their conviction rate is much higher. According to British Railway's Bye-law 17, indecent behaviour is prohibited on railway premises and in 1989 this led to the arrest of 226 men. A bye-law in the London Borough of Richmond makes it an offence to remain in a public toilet 'longer than is necessary'. In the spring of 1989, more than 150 men were charged with this offence.

The police are nowadays also resurrecting ancient and previously unused statutes to prosecute homosexual indecency. These statutes include the 1847 Town Police Clauses Act, the 1860 Ecclesiastical Courts Jurisdiction Act, and the old common law offence of 'outraging public decency' — none of which specifically refer to homosexuality or were legislated for the purpose of suppressing gay and bisexual men.

Public order laws, which were likewise never meant for the control of people's sexuality, are more and more being used against same-sex offenders. In October 1989, a 33-year-old gay man, Joseph Stewart, was fined £50 by Aberdeen Crown Court on the grounds that his wearing of women's clothing in a red light district late at night constituted behaviour likely to cause a breach of the peace.[6]

Section 5 of the 1986 Public Order Act, which was originally introduced to protect the public from rioters and football hooligans, has also been used to similar effect. Two 19 year olds — chef Andrew Cotton and cashier Philip Anderson — were both fined £40 in April 1988 for kissing each other in a London street. Passing judgement at Bow Street Court, Sir David Hopkin, the Chief Metropolitan Magistrate for London, ruled that they had contravened Section 5 of the Public Order Act which prohibits 'threatening...or disorderly behaviour' likely to cause public 'harassment, alarm or distress'.[7]

The level of criminalization of gay and bisexual men under these various laws is revealed in the Home Office publication, *Criminal Statistics England & Wales, Supplementary Tables Volumes 1-4, 1989*. Research on these figures has shown that in 1989 the overwhelmingly consensual gay offences of buggery, soliciting, indecency and procuring — plus estimated homosexual indecency offences under bye-laws etc. which are not included in the official figures — resulted in 3,900 prosecutions, 3,000 convictions, 500 cautions and over 200 imprisonments. Of these, consensual offences between men over the age of 16 accounted for approximately 3,500 prosecutions, 2,700 convictions, 380 cautions and 40-50 prison sentences.[8] Hardly any of these men would have been arrested if their partner had been a woman. The cost of prosecuting and imprisoning them is calculated to have been around £13 million.[9]

The 3,000 convictions in 1989 break down as follows:

- 1,503 convictions for indecency (mostly gay sex in non-private places)
- 462 convictions for soliciting (cruising and chatting up men)
- 346 convictions for procuring (inviting and aiding and abetting homosexual relations)
- 254 convictions for buggery (mainly age of consent violations with willing teenage men aged 13-21)
- 500 convictions (estimate) for homosexual indecency under miscellaneous statutes such as bye-laws, public order legislation and common law (mostly sex between men in parks, toilets and lover's lanes).[10]

The existence of institutionalized police and judicial homophobia has been revealed by my research, based on official Home Office statistics for 1989. Published in summary form under the title *Criminal Injustice*,[11] the main findings of this research are that:

- 30 per cent of all convictions for sexual offences are for consensual gay behaviour — although this behaviour comprises only 13 per cent of total recorded sex offences.
- Men who commit consenting homosexual acts are four times more likely to be convicted than men who commit heterosexual and violent sex offences.
- The average police clear-up rate for the mainly consensual gay offences of buggery, procuring and indecency is 97 per cent, which is 28 per cent higher than the average clear-up rate for rape and indecent assault on a woman. This extraordinarily high clear-up rate for victimless homosexual offences is suggestive of a police vendetta against the gay community.
- Compared with men who have consenting sex with girls under 16, men who commit the consensual offence of 'indecency between males' with partners over 16 are five times more likely to be prosecuted, and three times less likely to be let off with a caution.

- Convictions for victimless homosexual indecency rose by 106 per cent between 1985-89. According to the Home Office, this can be partly explained by the decision of some chief constables to 'target' these offences. Comparable heterosexual behaviour is rarely, if ever, targeted by the police.
- As a result, the number of convictions for consenting homosexual indecency was nearly four times greater in 1989 than in 1966 — the year before the supposed decriminalization of male homosexuality.
- Men who have consenting sex with 13-16-year-old boys nearly always get charged with 'indecent assault' (despite the boys being willing participants); whereas an 'indecent assault' charge is almost never bought against men who have consensual sex with girls in the same age range.
- Prison sentences for consenting homosexual relations with men aged 16-21 are sometimes as long as for rape, and often twice as long as the gaol terms for 'unlawful sexual intercourse' with a girl aged 13-16.

Despite decriminalization on the UK mainland, all homosexual relations between consenting adults remain a criminal offence in the self-governing British territories of the Isle of Man and Gibraltar, with anal sex still carrying a maximum sentence of life imprisonment in both places.

Two other UK-dependent territories have lifted their complete prohibition of homosexuality in recent years. In 1983, Guernsey decriminalized private sexual acts between consenting men aged 21 and over on a trial basis. This temporary decriminalization was extended indefinitely in 1986. Jersey followed suit in 1990, repealing its long-standing laws against sodomy.

Armed Forces & Merchant Navy

For military personnel, both homosexual orientation and behaviour are illegal. To be lesbian or gay, even if the person never has sex, is grounds for dismissal. Homosexual relations are punishable by up to two years imprisonment — followed by 'dismissal with disgrace' — under the service discipline regulations which forbid 'disgraceful conduct of a cruel, indecent, or unnatural kind' and 'conduct or neglect to the prejudice of good order and military discipline'.[12] These penalties apply in all circumstances, including cases where the homosexual behaviour takes place with civilians outside of barracks during leave time.

In 1990, 78 lesbian and gay service personnel were dismissed from the armed forces because of their homosexuality. Six of these personnel were court-martialled and imprisoned — three of them for 18 months — for committing homosexual acts which would not be an offence under civilian law.[13]

Examples of recent military witch-hunts against lesbian and gay service personnel include:

- In 1991, a woman serving in the Royal Navy reported that she had been investigated as a suspected lesbian simply because her name was discovered in another woman's address book. She recalls: 'I had my telephone tapped, I was followed off camp, my mail was "accidentally" opened, and I suffered stress at work with comments about "poofs, raving homosexuals and dykes"'.[14]

- A bandsman in the Royal Highland Fusiliers, Paul Crone, was imprisoned and tortured by Military Police in 1988 after he was seen talking to a gay former soldier while socializing off-duty. To make Crone to confess to his gayness, they subjected him to sleep deprivation, despoiling of his food, and forced physical exercises while being beaten. Military Police also stood on his back wearing boots with metal studs which cut into his flesh. According to a friend: 'For over a week, he couldn't wear a shirt without the blood seeping through'. Faced with incessant violent abuse, Crone admitted his homosexuality and was dismissed from the forces.[15]

- A corporal in the Women's Royal Army Corps (WRACS) was interrogated for eight hours and imprisoned for a week in 1989 after officers from the Special Investigation Bureau (SIB) barged into her quarters while she was innocently watching television with another woman soldier. Accusing her of being a lesbian, but unable to prove the charges, the

SIB pressured and harassed her until she eventually agreed to resign.[16]

- In 1987, second aircraftsmen Andy Thomas and Ian Smith were court-martialled, and received custodial sentences of four and three months respectively, for consensual sex during their free time at RAF Akrotiri in Cyprus.[17]

In the merchant navy it is a criminal offence for a seaman to have sex with another man on board a UK-registered vessel, even in private with a consenting adult during off-duty hours.

Employment Discrimination

The law offers lesbians and gay men no protection from discrimination. It is therefore legal, by default, to discriminate against homosexuals in employment, housing, education, and the provision of other public and private services.

Employment-related discrimination is particularly serious and has been officially-sanctioned by Industrial Tribunals. This means that lesbians and gay men have no job security. They can be demoted or dismissed at the whim of their employers, irrespective of their length and quality of service.

- In 1990, Lord Dervaird was forced to resign his position as a senior Scottish judge following allegations of homosexuality.[18]
- In 1989, an auxiliary nurse, James Greenam, was refused a job with the Homecare nursing agency after they discovered he was gay.[19]
- In 1988, the Lescleave Hotel in Cornwall sacked its head chef, Carol Harris, allegedly on the grounds that her lesbianism would be bad for business.[20]
- In 1987, Andrew Hodges lost his appeal against dismissal from the Government Communications Headquarters (GCHQ) after his civil service employers claimed that his gay lifestyle and openness about his homosexuality would make him a security risk.[21]

Other forms of homophobic discrimination include the decision of Haringey Council in 1989 to exclude information for lesbian and gay young people from a local library exhibition, *Education in the Nineties*;[22] the 1987 Leeds College of Music ban on lesbian and gay society advertisements on college noticeboards;[23] the rejection of a joint housing application from two gay partners by Doncaster Council in 1986;[24] and the Royal College of Nursing's refusal in 1989 to sanction the establishment of a support group for lesbian union members.[25]

Incitement to Hatred

Lesbians and gay men have no protection comparable to the Race Relations Act which outlaws incitement to hatred on the grounds of a person's race. In the absence of any laws to stop people from inciting hatred against lesbians and gay men, it is *de facto* lawful to stir up prejudice against homosexuals.

The tabloid press, while it would never use the words 'nigger' or 'yid', regularly refers to lesbians and gay men as 'lezzies', 'queers' and 'poofs'. It also frequently uses pejorative adjectives like 'depraved', 'perverse', 'sordid', 'bizarre' and 'sick' to describe homosexuals. On 17 May 1991, the *Daily Star* ridiculed lesbian and gay service personnel, some of whom had only weeks earlier risked their lives in the Gulf War, as 'Poofters on Parade'. It also vilified those advocating the decriminalization of homosexual relations for military personnel as 'strident, mincing preachers of filth'. In a similar hateful vein, *The Sun* had earlier attacked gay clergy as 'Pulpit Poofs' in its front page headline on 12 November 1987.

These homophobic news stories have a cumulative effect. They contribute to hostile public perceptions of lesbians and gay men and thereby indirectly fuel popular prejudice, discrimination and violence against the lesbian and gay community.

In the five years, 1986-91 inclusive, more than 70 gay and bisexual men were murdered — many by queer-bashers motivated by anti-gay hatred.[26] Every year, thousands more gay men and lesbians are estimated to be assaulted, threatened and abused because of their sexuality. A survey published by the London Gay Teenage Group in 1984, found that 60 per cent of the lesbian and gay teenagers questioned had experienced verbal abuse because of their sexuality. Another survey, conducted by the Gay London Policing Group in 1989, found that 40 per cent of gay men and 25 per cent of lesbians interviewed had been violently attacked in the recent past.

Immigration & Residence Rights

The foreign partners of British lesbians and gay men have no right to immigrate and establish permanent residence in the UK with their lovers, regardless of the length and stability of their relationship.

In October 1988, an Australian lesbian, Christine Moss, who had been living in the UK with her British partner for five years, had her appeal to remain in the UK rejected by the Home Office. She was forced to leave the country a few months later.[27]

In another case, an Irish gay man living permanently in London petitioned the Home Office in 1986 to grant residence rights in the UK to his Portuguese lover of six years standing. He argued that European Community regulations and the European Convention on Human Rights entitled him to establish a family with his male partner. However, the Home Office ruled that the right to form a family does not cover same-sex relationships and that it is under no legal obligation to treat homosexual partners the same as heterosexual ones.[28]

Political Asylum

The British government has, on several occasions, refused to grant political asylum to homosexuals fearing persecution in their home countries. A Cypriot gay man sought asylum in the UK in 1989 on the grounds that he risked imprisonment if he returned to Cyprus where homosexuality is totally illegal. His request for residence in Britain was turned down by the Home Secretary who, while acknowledging that homosexual acts are punishable by imprisonment in Cyprus, stated that 'statistically the risk did not seem to be very great, and even where there was prosecution the consequences were not particularly dire'. (The maximum penalty for homosexuality in Cyprus is 5 years gaol.)

On appeal, Mr Justice Kennedy upheld the Home Secretary's decision. He said that if the man was arrested for homosexual behaviour on his return to Cyprus, it would 'not amount to persecution'. Rather, it would be his own fault for having sex with men in the knowledge that it was against the law. Concluding that the man would be at no risk of prosecution if he abstained from gay relationships, the judge rejected the man's appeal for asylum.[29]

Censorship

British censorship laws are among the most homophobic in Europe. Lesbian and gay-themed books, videos and magazines which are freely available in most countries on the continent are often banned from publication or sale in the UK, and from importation from abroad.

Censorship is enforced much more harshly against homo-erotic photography, literature, art and film, than against comparable heterosexual material. A photo-montage by student Paul Wolfe, which depicted two uniformed sailors kissing with their genitals exposed, was removed from Nottingham Polytechnic's 1991 fine arts degree catalogue by the college authorities; yet it's highly doubtful that similar heterosexual subject matter would have been censored in the same way.[30] The import of the gay sex education manual, *Men Loving Men*, is effectively banned; whereas equivalent heterosexual guides, such as *The Joy of Sex*, can be freely brought into the country.

The restriction on the availability of explicit homosexual material from abroad is enforced under the sweeping anti-obscenity provisions of the 1876 Customs Consolidation Act. Using this legislation, in 1984 Customs officers raided Gay's The Word bookshop in London and intercepted its mail, seizing hundreds of gay books imported into this country from overseas. The volumes seized on the grounds of obscenity included works by Robin Maugham, Jean Genet, Allen Ginsberg, Gore Vidal, Jean-Paul Sartre and Tennessee Williams (some of which were already lawfully published and on sale in the UK).[31]

In 1989, Customs intercepted correspondence to *Capital Gay* newspaper in London, confiscating a copy of *De Gay Krant*, the respected Dutch lesbian and gay community publication, on the grounds that it was 'indecent'.[32]

Even erotic material designed to educate people about HIV prevention is not exempt. A consignment of 'safer sex' posters imported from Germany by London Lesbian & Gay Switchboard was seized in June 1991.[33]

Other examples of homophobic censorship include:

- In 1987, the BBC ordered changes in the script of the television series *Eastenders*, deleting a hug and cuddle between on-screen gay lovers, Colin and Barry.[34]
- A year later, a scene in the rival Channel Four soap, *Brookside*, which featured two gay characters in bed together, was also axed.[35]
- Hull City Council banned a showing in 1989 of the Jean Genet film, *Un Chant d'Amour*, because of its 'very explicit scenes of homosexuality' (though these scenes are a good deal less explicit than many heterosexual films with an '18' certificate).[36]
- The newsagent chain-store John Menzies, in 1991, instructed all its branches not to stock copies of the Marquis de Sade book *120 Days of Sodom*;[37] though it later rescinded this instruction following public criticism and protests.

Lesbian & Gay Partnerships

The law does not recognize committed homosexual relationships. Lesbian and gay partners therefore have no legal rights with regard to pensions, inheritance, tenancy, compassionate leave, or next-of-kin visiting rights in hospitals and prisons.

Housing law is typical of this non-recognition of same-sex partnerships. In the early 1980s, Nicki Rodrigo and Mary Simpson were lovers. They lived together in Rodrigo's council flat in Harrogate. Shortly after Rodrigo's death, Simpson was evicted from the flat by Harrogate Council. Because the tenancy was in Rodrigo's name, the council argued that Simpson had no right to continue living in the premises. In December 1985, the Appeal Court upheld Harrogate's eviction order. It ruled that the 1980 Housing Act, which gives the surviving partner of a relationship the right to inherit the tenancy, does not apply to lesbian and gay couples.[38]

Child Access & Custody

There are no official legal restrictions on lesbian mothers and gay fathers having access to, or custody of, their children following divorce from their spouse. In practice, however, judges often rule that a 'normal family life' is essential for the well-being of a child and that a parent's lesbianism or gayness renders them 'unsuitable' to have access to, or custody of, their children (even in cases where the child concerned has expressed the wish to remain with a lesbian or gay parent).

In 1989, Lord Cowrie judged that a lesbian mother should lose custody of her nine-year-old son who had lived with her since she had divorced and separated from her husband eight years earlier. Lord Cowrie upheld the earlier decision of Lord Davidson who had argued that by living with his lesbian mother, the boy would face 'unusual difficulties' as he grew up and that he would risk embarrassment and distress on learning of his mother's relationship with another woman.[39]

Supervision & Care Orders

The legal requirement for local authorities to protect children from 'moral danger' sometimes results in supervision or care orders being used to prevent teenagers who are lesbian and gay from expressing their sexual and emotional feelings.

In June 1987, 16-year-old Craig Diver was kept in care against his will by a Scottish children's panel following reports that he frequented gay clubs and had gay relationships.[40]

The related legal requirement to 'promote the welfare of children' is rarely invoked to protect the thousands of lesbian and gay young people who are abused and beaten by their homophobic parents and who, in extreme cases, are driven to depression and attempted suicide. Of the young lesbians and gay men surveyed by the London Gay Teenage Group in 1984: one in five had attempted suicide, one in ten had been thrown out of home by their parents, and one in seven had been sent to a psychiatrist because of their sexuality.

Fostering & Adoption of Children

Lesbian and gay couples, even those in long-term stable relationships, are banned from adopting children. In reply to a parliamentary question on 25 January 1990, the Secretary of State for Health, Virginia Bottomley, stated: 'The law does not allow two people to adopt unless they are married'.

There are no such restrictions on the fostering of children by homosexuals, whether as individuals or as couples. Nevertheless, some local authorities, such as Wandsworth and Brent, refuse to foster children with lesbians and gay men (even when they have the best parenting skills and home environment to offer).[41]

Sex Education

Under Section 46 of the 1986 Education Act, sex education lessons must encourage pupils 'to have due regard to moral considerations and the value of family life'. A follow-up circular (No.11/87), issued by the Department of Education and Science on 25 September 1987, states that sex education lessons must be 'set within a clear moral framework...There is no place in any school in any circumstances for teaching which advocates homosexual behaviour, which presents it as the "norm", or which encourages homosexual experimentation by pupils'.

These constraints tend to discourage coverage of homosexuality in sex education classes — denying pupils a full understanding of human sexuality and ignoring the needs of those who are struggling to come to terms with their homosexuality. A 1991 survey of 16-19 year olds by the Health Education Authority found that over 80 per cent had received no information in school about lesbian and gay sexuality in their sex education lessons at school.[42]

Restrictions on Promotion

According to Section 28 of the Local Government Act 1988, it is illegal for a local authority to 'intentionally promote homosexuality' or to promote the teaching in schools of 'the acceptability of homosexuality as a pretended family relationship'.

Since it has come into effect, Section 28 has encouraged at least 35 instances of self-censorship by local authorities fearful of prosecution. These have included the refusal of Hereford and Worcester County Council to fund a lesbian community newsletter; the cancellation of a school performance of the Avon Touring Theatre's gay-themed play, *Trapped in Time*; the attempt by councils in Strathclyde and Essex to ban student lesbian and gay societies from meeting on college premises; and the rejection by Edinburgh District Council of a grant application from the Scottish Homosexual Action Group towards the cost of a poetry and music festival.[43]

In July 1988, the government introduced a potentially even more sweeping 'morality clause' into its Code of Recommended Practice on Local Authority Publicity. Section 17 states: 'Publicity should not attack, nor appear to undermine, generally accepted moral standards'.[44]

1   *The Sun*, 19 and 20 September 1991.
    Today, 21 September 1991.
    Capital Gay, 15 November 1991.
2   Home Office Statistics Division and Press Office, fax dated 27 February 1991.
3   *Criminal Statistics England & Wales*, Supplementary Tables 1989, Volumes 1-4, Government Statistical Office, HMSO, November 1990.
4   *Capital Gay*, 15 November 1985.
5   *The Pink Paper*, 22 July 1989.
6   *The Pink Paper*, 14 October 1989.
    The Scotsman, 3 May 1990.
7   *Capital Gay*, 29 April 1988.
8   *The Pink Paper*, 26 October 1991.
9   *Capital Gay*, 24 May and 14 June 1991.
10 *Capital Gay*, 28 June 1991.

11 *The Pink Paper*, 26 October 1991.

12 Army Act 1955 (Sections 66 & 69), Air Force Act 1955 (Section 66), and Naval Discipline Act 1957 (Section 37).

13 Earl of Arran, Parliamentary Under-Secretary of State for Defence for the Armed Forces, letters to Harry Cohen, MP dated 14 March and 21 May 1991.

14 *The Independent*, 12 June 1991.

15 *The Independent*, 26 August 1991.

16 *Capital Gay*, 26 April 1991.

17 *HIM*, No. 45, February 1991.

18 *The Independent*, 18 January 1990.

19 *The Pink Paper*, 18 February 1989.

20 *Capital Gay*, 4 March 1988.

21 *The Pink Paper*, 12 and 19 November 1987.

22 *Capital Gay*, 17 November 1989.

23 *The Pink Paper*, 26 May 1988.

24 *OUT*, No. 28, February/March 1986.

25 *The Pink Paper*, 18 February 1989.

26 *Gay Times,* October 1990, and subsequent research by David Smith.

27 *Capital Gay*, 14 October 1988.

28 *The Pink Paper*, 15 December 1990.

29 *The Pink Paper*, 5 August 1989.

30 *The Guardian*, 2 July 1991.

31 *The Guardian*, 25 and 27 June 1985.
   Capital Gay, 14 March and 14 July 1986.

32 *Capital Gay*, 16 June 1989.

33 *Capital Gay*, 9 August 1991.

34 *Capital Gay*, 13 November 1987.

35 *The Pink Paper*, 21 April 1988.

36 *The Pink Paper*, 11 February 1989.

37 *Capital Gay*, 23 August 1991.

38 *The Guardian*, 1 March 1985.

39 *The Pink Paper*, 28 October 1989.

40 *Capital Gay*, 26 June 1987.

41 *Capital Gay*, 2 August 1991.
   The Pink Paper, 31 August 1991.

42 *Capital Gay*, 16 August 1991.

43 *The Pink Paper*, 20 October 1988.
   The Guardian, 11 October 1989.

44 *The Pink Paper*, 27 October 1988.

Guide to Other
European Countries

ALBANIA

Homosexuality has not been mentioned in the penal code since 1977. Section 239, which penalized all sex between men with up to ten years imprisonment, was deleted in that year. This resulted in a common age of consent of 14 for everyone, according to Sections 97-100 of the penal code. Paradoxically, the maximum penalty for men having sex with under age girls is 15 years imprisonment, whereas for sex with boys under 14 it is only five years.[1]

Despite formal legal equality, there remain strong social taboos against homosexuality. This is due to nearly half a century of authoritarian and puritanical Communism, plus the country's long history of Islamic influence. As a result, there is no visible or organized lesbian and gay community; though this is likely to change in the wake of the post-Communist democratization process and the country's growing contacts with western Europe.

1 *Homosexualität im Europa*, Hosi Wien, 1989, p. 6.
   Second ILGA Pink Book, Utrecht University, 1988, p. 225.

AUSTRIA

Both lesbianism and gayness were totally forbidden until 1971 when male and female homosexual acts were legalized for the first time. An age of consent of 18 was introduced for gay men, while for lesbians it was set at 14, in line with the age for heterosexuals.[1] In 1989, gay prostitution was legalized on the same basis as its heterosexual equivalent.

Section 220 of the penal code continues to make it unlawful to publicly advocate, promote or encourage homosexual acts — carrying a maximum penalty of six months in gaol. This law was used to justify the Austrian Supreme Court's ruling that explicit representations of homosexual acts constitute hard-core pornography and are therefore illegal. Under Section 221, those who establish or belong to an organization which supports 'homosexual lewdness' and which causes public offence are also liable to six months imprisonment.[2]

These two laws were originally introduced during the period of Nazi occupation and were never repealed. They mean that lesbian and gay organizations and publications are technically illegal. Though there have been several cases where lesbian and gay activists have been charged under Sections 220 and 221, these charges have usually later been dropped. A recent exception was in 1990 when the directors of the Austrian lesbian and gay organization, Hosi Wien, were convicted under Section 220 of 'promoting homosexuality'. They were charged after Hosi Wien's youth group sent copies of the gay news and information magazines, *Tabu* and *Lambda-Nachrichten*, to secondary schools in 1988. The magazine was deemed to have promoted homosexuality on three counts: carrying gay contact ads, featuring a positive review of the American gay movie *Parting Glances*, and publicizing the names of famous homosexuals in Austrian history. Following the controversy surrounding this case, the Minister of Justice announced that Sections 220 and 221 will be repealed in a future revision of the country's criminal code.[3] Indeed, a Bill to this effect has already been drafted and these Sections are expected to be abolished in 1992.

Homosexuals are permitted to serve in the armed forces; though they are forbidden to have sexual relations with subordinates, or with others inside barracks or during duty hours.[4]

Political asylum has occasionally been granted to homosexuals fearing persecution in their home countries. However, this is unofficial and at the authorities discretion rather than being a statutory right. In 1984 and 1986, Austrian officials gave refugee status to two gay men from Iran, arguing that the Geneva Convention on Refugees is applicable in cases where individuals are liable to persecution because of their homosexuality.[5]

In 1988, a Ministry of Justice proposal to lower the age of consent for gay men from 18 to 16 was vetoed by the Minister for the Environment, Family and Youth.

1   *Second ILGA Pink Book*, Utrecht University, 1988, p. 225.
2   Ibid.
3   *Gay Times*, November 1990 and July 1991.
4   *Homosexual Men & Women in the Armed Forces*, ILGA, 1987.
5   *Iceberg Report*, Utrecht University, 1990, p. 78.

BELGIUM

In 1792, male gay behaviour was decriminalized. Until 1846, there was no age of consent. From 1846 to 1912, the age of consent was 14 for heterosexuals and homosexuals alike. In 1912, it was raised to 16 years. A discriminatory age of consent for gay men was introduced for the first time in 1965. Set at 18 years, it remained in force for two decades. In 1985, a common age of consent of 16 for heterosexuals, lesbians and gay men was finally enacted.[1]

Though Belgian society is fairly tolerant towards homosexuals, cases of police harassment still periodically occur. In August 1989, officers raiding a gay disco in search of drugs strip-searched, assaulted and detained overnight many of the club-goers.

While there is no official recognition of same-sex relationships, individual corporations are gradually introducing rights for homosexual employees and their partners. In 1990, the Belgian Telephone and Post Service extended eligibility for corporate benefits to the partners of its employees, including both heterosexual spouses and homosexual lovers.[2] The following year, two gay prisoners in an Antwerp gaol won the right to have 'conjugal visits' from their lovers, on the same basis as is granted to heterosexual prisoners and their spouses.[3]

The government is currently considering proposals for anti-discrimination legislation and laws against incitement to hatred. These are expected to be enacted within the next couple of years.

Homosexuality is no bar against a person enlisting in the armed forces.[4]

1   *Homosexualität im Europa,* Hosi Wien, 1989, p. 6-7.
2   *Gay Times,* February 1990.
3   *The Pink Paper,* 19 October 1991.
4   *Homosexual Men & Women in the Armed Forces,* ILGA, 1987.

BULGARIA

Until 1968, both male and female homosexuality were completely prohibited. Since then, the age of consent has been 18 for lesbians and gay men, compared with 14 for heterosexuals. According to Article 157 of the penal code, the maximum penalty for under age homosexual relations is five years imprisonment.[1]

Despite legalization, the public expression of sexual desire or affection between people of the same sex of any age remains a serious punishable offence under the laws that prohibit behaviour which 'causes scandal or entices others to perversity'.[2]

Ruled by a moralistic Communist government for 40 years, Bulgaria is a sexually repressive society. Meeting places for homosexuals are few in number. There is widespread ignorance and prejudice against lesbianism and gayness.

Since 1990, the emerging free press has begun to publish feature stories about homosexuality. However, some of these have been very homophobic and have resulted in a big increase in queer-bashing attacks.

An informal gay group began organizing at Sofia University in late 1990, and the first gay club opened in 1991.

1   *Second ILGA Pink Book,* Utrecht University, 1988, p. 227-8
2   Ibid.

CYPRUS

All homosexual acts between men were outlawed in the nineteenth century when the island was under British colonial rule. In 1929, a new criminal code was introduced. Under Article 171, which still remains in force, 'carnal knowledge of any person against the order of nature' is illegal. Offenders are liable to five years imprisonment. Even attempted homosexual relations are a crime and carry a three year sentence. For heterosexual men, there is no age of consent. For women, the minimum age is 16 years.[1]

Gay men are not allowed to serve in the military. According to the Ministry of Justice: 'Homosexual men are exempted from the obligation to serve in the National Guard of Cyprus on health grounds'.[2]

Homosexuality is not part of the sex education curriculum, which tends to be restricted to factual information about human reproduction.

Hardly any lesbians or gay men are public about their sexuality for fear of ridicule and discrimination. And with good reason. The Archbishop of the Cypriot Orthodox Church declared in 1990 that homosexuals and homosexual sympathizers would be excommunicated and refused church funeral and burial services.[3]

In December 1990, the European Commission on Human Rights agreed that the Cypriot government's ban on homosexual relations was a violation of the right to privacy under Article 8 of the ECHR. As a result, the government of Cyprus is expected to decriminalize male homosexuality in the near future.[4]

1   Director-General of the Ministry of Justice in Cyprus, letter to Peter Tatchell dated 20 January 1990.
2   Ibid.
3   *Capital Gay*, 11 January 1991.
4   *Gay Times*, January 1991.

CZECHOSLOVAKIA

In 1961, lesbianism and gayness were legalized, but with a discriminatory age of consent. Section 244 of the penal code specified the minimum age for same-sex contacts at 18 years, as opposed to 15 for heterosexual relations. In July 1990, following the democratic revolution, the age of consent for lesbians and gay men was lowered to 15 to bring it into line with that for men and women. Male prostitution was also decriminalized.[1]

During the era of Communist rule, Czechoslovakia was one of the first Eastern-bloc countries to liberalize its official attitudes towards lesbians and gay men. For most of the post-war period, the Communist authorities tolerated the existence of discreet gay bars and open-air cruising. From the mid-1980s, both the state television station and the state-run daily newspaper for youth, *Mlada-Fronta*, featured positive discussions about homosexual issues.

While informal lesbian and gay groups have existed unofficially since 1981, the first official homosexual rights organization, Lambda Praha, was only publicly launched in the spring of 1988. Its dialogue with officials from the then Communist government generated a reasonably sympathetic response. Following the overthrow of the Communist regime in late 1989, representatives from the new democratic Czechoslovak parliament met with lesbian and gay activists. An equal age of consent was legislated shortly afterwards. Consideration is currently being given to demands for the legal recognition of same-sex partnerships and the granting of political asylum to homosexuals who flee anti-gay persecution.[2]

In the June 1990 general election an openly gay candidate, Jiri Hromada, stood unsuccessfully for the independent political bloc, the Movement for Civic Freedom.

The lesbian and gay movement is now organized in all major Czech cities. Its newspaper, *Lambda*, has a circulation of 4,000. In the Slovak republic, there is a parallel homosexual rights organization known as Ganymedes.

1   *Gay Times*, February 1991, p. 37-9.
2   Ibid.

DENMARK

The ban on male homosexual acts was lifted in 1930; though not until 1976 was a common age of consent of 15 finally introduced under Article 222 of the criminal code (in cases where the older person is a guardian or teacher, the age of consent is 18).[1]

In 1984, the national parliament, the Folketing, set up a commission to recommend proposals to combat discrimination against lesbians and gay men. This led, in 1987, to the passing of an anti-discrimination statute, Article 289, which protects homosexuals from discrimination in the provision of goods and services and guarantees equal access to public facilities. The penalty for infringements is a fine or imprisonment up to six months.[2]

The commission of inquiry also resulted in the enactment in 1987 of laws against incitement to hatred on the grounds of a person's sexuality. Article 266a reads:

> 'Any person who, publicly or with the intention of wider dissemination, makes a statement or imparts other information by which a group of people are threatened, insulted or degraded on account of their race, colour, national or ethnic origin, religion or sexual orientation, shall be liable to a fine, or to simple detention, or to imprisonment for any term not exceeding two years'.[3]

In the first step towards the recognition of homosexual partnerships, in 1986 it was decreed that lesbian and gay couples could inherit from each other. Three years later, the Danish Registered Partnership Act of 1989 was passed. It extends the principle of civil marriage to same-sex couples, allowing them to register their relationship and receive official recognition and legal entitlements on a par with married men and women. Under this law, homosexual partners enjoy equal rights with married heterosexual people in respect to inheritance, taxation, alimony, pensions and, in the case of foreign partners, the right of permanent residency in the country. The only exception is their ineligibility to jointly adopt children. In the first few months of the new law, 1,700 lesbian and gay couples registered their relationships, accounting for one in five of all civil marriages during that period.[4]

Since 1979, homosexuals have been allowed to join the armed forces.[5]

According to Article 19 of the Aliens Law, a foreign person cohabiting for a prolonged duration with a partner who is permanently residing in Denmark is entitled to a permit to remain in the country, irrespective of whether the relationship is of a heterosexual or homosexual character.[6] Under Articles 7 and 9 of the same legislation, foreign homosexuals at risk of victimization by their own governments are eligible for political asylum.[7]

Denmark is probably the most liberal country in all of Europe, with a high level of legal protection and social acceptance of lesbians and gay men. There is regular and supportive liaison between the government and the homosexual community.

1   *Homosexualität im Europa*, Hosi Wien, 1989, p. 6.
2   *Iceberg Report*, Utrecht University, 1990, p. 44.
3   Ibid., p. 65.
4   *Capital Gay*, 25 May, 1990.
5   *Homosexual Men & Women in the Armed Forces*, ILGA, 1987.
6   *Iceberg Report*, Utrecht University, 1990, p. 28.
7   Ibid., p. 77.

ESTONIA

Following the forcible incorporation of Estonia into the Soviet Union in 1940, the Soviet anti-sodomy laws became part of the penal code. Article 118 punishes homosexual intercourse with up to five years hard labour. However, there are few prosecutions and official decriminalization is expected soon as part of a post-independence revision of the penal code. The age of consent for heterosexuals is 16.[1]

Throughout the period of rule from Moscow, Estonia and the other two Baltic republics were always the most westernized and liberal parts of the USSR — largely due to their long-standing cultural ties with the progressive Scandinavian countries and their ability to receive television and radio broadcasts from abroad.

This more liberal atmosphere led, in May 1990, to Estonian lesbian and gay activists organizing the Soviet Union's first ever conference on homosexual issues. With the theme of 'Sexual

Minorities and Society: Changing Attitudes to Homosexuality',
the conference was held at the Institute of History in the capital,
Tallinn, and was attended by activists and academics from other
parts of the USSR and from Western Europe.[2]

1 Kurt Krickler/Hosi Wien, October 1991.
House of Commons Library, Research Division, September 1991.
2 *Gay Times*, July 1990.

FINLAND

Before 1971, both lesbian and gay sexual acts had always been
illegal. Though now decriminalized, the age of consent for
homosexual men and women is fixed at 18; two years higher
than the minimum age of 16 for heterosexuals. A special age of
consent of 21 applies to same-sex relations where there is a
relationship of dependency, such as between a teacher and a
student. For equivalent heterosexual acts, the special age of
consent is three years younger (18).[1]

Whereas violations of the age of consent by heterosexuals
include the option of punishment by a fine only, breaches by
homosexuals automatically carry a prison sentence up to a
maximum of three years.[2]

Until 1981, homosexuality was officially classified as a mental
disorder.[3]

Today, homosexuality is not contrary to military regulations
and gay men are free to serve in the armed forces.[4]

Lesbian and gay partnerships are only recognized in the
limited field of social welfare benefits; though the city of
Helsinki in 1991 agreed that lesbian and gay couples would be
treated the same as childless heterosexual couples with respect
to eligibility for municipal housing.

The promotion of homosexuality is unlawful under Section
20:9.2 of the penal code. It forbids the 'public encouragement
of fornication between members of the same sex.' Though the
lesbian and gay movement operates quite freely, this law technically renders it illegal and creates a climate of intimidation. In
the 1970s, Section 20:9.2 was used to censor programmes about
lesbians and gay men. The film *Sunday Bloody Sunday* was banned

from television because it was thought to promote homosexuality. Likewise, television programme makers were threatened with prosecution following the transmission of documentaries about discrimination against lesbians and gay men in Finland, and about lesbian and gay Christians in the United States.[5]

1 Olli Stalstrom of SETA (Finnish lesbian and gay rights organization), letter to Peter Tatchell dated 3 February 1990.
2 Ibid.
3 Ibid.
4 Ibid.
5 Ibid.

FRANCE

Prior to 1791, there was a complete prohibition on male homosexuality. After 1791, and until 1832, there was no age of consent. Between 1832 and 1863, the minimum age was 11 for everyone, regardless of sexual orientation. In 1863, this was raised to 13 years. During the last war, in 1942, the pro-Nazi Vichy regime introduced an age of consent of 21 for gay men. This remained in force after liberation until 1978 when it was reduced to 18. Finally, in 1982, 38 years after the fall of the Vichy dictatorship, the Socialist government of François Mitterrand brought the age of consent for gay men down to 15, equalizing it with the age for heterosexuals which had been enacted by the post-war French government in 1945. The sexual offences section of the penal code now no longer mentions homosexuality.[1]

Anti-discrimination laws were introduced in 1985. Though not explicitly giving protection on the basis of sexual orientation, the grounds of *moeurs* (meaning morals and lifestyle) have been interpreted as including homosexuality. This means that lesbian and gay individuals are protected against discrimination in employment and in access to goods and services. The penalty for infringements is up to a year in gaol and/or a fine of 20,000 francs.[2]

Homosexuality is not a barrier to membership of the armed forces, nor a disciplinary offence.[3]

In 1989, the Supreme Court rejected a claim by a homosexual couple seeking the same legal entitlements as unmarried heterosexual couples.

1   *Homosexualität im Europa*, Hosi Wien, 1989, p. 6-8.
2   *Iceberg Report*, Utrecht University, 1990, p. 37.
3   *Homosexual Men & Women in the Armed Forces*, ILGA, 1987.

GERMANY

In 1871, during the rule of Chancellor Otto von Bismarck, male homosexuality was declared illegal under Paragraph 175 of the penal code (lesbianism has never been criminalized in German law).

A long campaign for the repeal of Paragraph 175 was initiated in 1897 by the left-wing Social Democrat and sexual reformer Dr Magnus Hirschfeld. This campaign gathered momentum in the early 1930s. However, it was brought to an abrupt halt with the advent of the Nazi regime in 1933. Soon after Hitler came to power, organizations advocating homosexual rights were banned, gay bars were closed down, and the first homosexuals were deported to concentration camps. By late 1934, the SS drew up its notorious 'pink lists' and mass round-ups began. A year later, more sweeping anti-gay laws were introduced and made retroactive. Under these decrees, the desire or intent to commit homosexual acts was deemed to be just as criminal as the acts themselves. In effect, homosexual thoughts were declared illegal. The head of the Gestapo, Heinrich Himmler, justified the Nazi genocide policy against homosexuals as 'the extermination of abnormal existence'.[1]

According to surviving Nazi records, at least 63,000 German homosexuals, including nearly 4,000 aged 14-18, were sentenced between 1933-44.[2] However, the real number was much higher. The Nazi records are incomplete and they do not include those who were summarily punished. Nor do they include those foreign homosexuals who were incarcerated in the Nazi-occupied countries. The true number of gay and bisexual men sent to prisons and concentration camps was probably closer to 100,000.

In the aftermath of the Second World War, two German states were created: East Germany in the Soviet-liberated sector and West Germany in the regions freed by the US-led armies.

The Communist state of East Germany was the first to lift the total ban on sex between men. In 1968, male homosexual acts were legalized, establishing an age of consent of 18 (four years higher than the minimum age of 14 for heterosexuals). A year later, West Germany followed suit. However, its decriminalization laws set the age of consent at 21 years, compared with 14 for heterosexuals. This was reduced to 18 in 1973. Today the age of consent for gay sex remains at 18 years — four years higher than the age for lawful sex between men and women.[3]

East Germany led again in 1989 when it lowered the age of consent for gay and bisexual men to 14, establishing a common age of consent for both heterosexuals and homosexuals. The only qualification was that sex with 14-18 year olds could be prosecuted, in certain circumstances, if it involved the exchange of money or the abuse of a position of authority.[4]

Since German reunification in 1990, there has existed an interim situation where East Germany's laws concerning homosexuality continue to apply in the eastern half of the country, and West Germany's legislation remains in force in the western half. In late 1991, the German government announced that it had drafted a Bill to equalize the age of consent at 16 for everyone. This Bill is expected to become law in 1992.[5]

The broader history of official attitudes towards same-sex relations in the two Germanies is also instructive. In West Germany, despite its democratic credentials and professed commitment to human rights, lesbians and gay men never enjoyed legal equality and were treated badly by comparison to their counterparts in the Netherlands and the Scandinavian countries.

Individual homosexuals were sometimes allowed to adopt children; though couples were barred from doing so. They could enlist in the armed forces, but were not allowed to become officers on the grounds that they might abuse their authority to seduce lower ranks (the same restriction also applied in East Germany).[6] Political asylum was occasionally granted to lesbian and gay people, from countries like Iran and Pakistan, who faced persecution because of their sexuality; however this was a purely discretionary policy.

In both West and East Germany, there were never any specific laws against anti-gay discrimination. However, both had general constitutional guarantees of human rights and equal treatment for all citizens which were supposed to give everyone — including, by implication, lesbians and gay men — protection against discrimination. In practice, these guarantees were often meaningless for homosexual people. The first attempt to remedy this lack of explicit constitutional protection for lesbians and gay men was made by the eastern German state of Brandenburg in 1991. It's new draft constitution prohibits discrimination on the grounds of 'sexual orientation'.

Compared with the West, East Germany had relatively little queer-bashing violence. There were few overtly homophobic politicians or newspapers. However, homosexuality was also less visible and organized. Indeed, the lesbian and gay movement which began to form in the East in the early 1980s was barely tolerated by the authorities and only won official acceptance towards the end of the decade, a couple of years before the fall of the Communist regime.

In East Germany, the first positive and supportive articles about homosexuality began to appear in the official press in the mid-1980s. Around the same time, discreet lesbian and gay contact ads were also accepted in the state-run newspapers. In January 1986, the official East German news agency, ADN, called for the social acceptance of lesbians and gay men and stressed the government's guarantee of equal treatment for all citizens, irrespective of their sexuality. Other government publicity criticized those who blamed homosexuals for the spread of HIV and called for compassion and solidarity with people with Aids. In 1988, the *GDR Review*, East Germany's official international public information magazine, reported positively on the activities of the Gerede youth club for lesbians and gay men in Dresden. It noted that self-acceptance by homosexual people is not just a question of homosexuals overcoming internalized guilt; it's also dependent on challenging social attitudes, in particular the prejudice of heterosexual people.

East Germany's first public conference on homosexuality was

held in Leipzig in 1985. Convened by sexologists and social scientists, it was also addressed by the lesbian activist Uschi Sillge, and by Eduard Stapel who was one of the founders of the first homosexual organization in the churches in 1982. By the late 1980s, there were 20 lesbian and gay groups affiliated with the Protestant churches and a dozen other lesbian and gay clubs, some of which were part of the official youth and Communist movements.

In February 1990, at a conference in Leipzig, many of these organizations decided to join together in a federation, the Schwulenverband der DDR. Its principle demands were for government reparations to the homosexual victims of Nazism, the official recognition of lesbian and gay partnerships, and the right of lesbian and gay couples to adopt children.

In the ten months between the collapse of the old Communist regime of Erich Honecker in late 1989, and German reunification in October 1990, round table discussions between the Communist government and the opposition resulted in radical proposals for lesbian and gay equality. These included constitutional guarantees to outlaw anti-homosexual discrimination; the creation of a Ministry for Equality with a lesbian and gay rights secretariat; the recognition of oppression because of one's homosexuality as a legitimate grounds for the awarding of political asylum; and the eligibility of same-sex partners to marry at a registry office and enjoy legal rights on an equal basis with heterosexual husbands and wives, including the right to foster and adopt children. These proposals fell following the dissolution of the East German state and the establishment of a united Germany.[7]

Since German reunification there has been an upsurge in neo-Nazi violence against lesbians and gay men, particularly in eastern Germany. In a series of attacks during 1990 and 1991 in eastern Berlin, extreme right-wingers beat up customers in a gay bar, wrecked a gay garden party, and violently assaulted gay disco-goers.

1   Richard Plant, *The Pink Triangle*, Mainstream, 1987.
2   Ibid., p. 230-2.
3   *Homosexualität im Europa*, Hosi Wien, 1989, p. 5-8.

Press Office, West German Embassy, London, letter to Peter Tatchell dated 26 February 1990.

4 Christian Pulz of the East German lesbian and gay movement, interviewed by Peter Tatchell, March 1990.

5 *Capital Gay*, 15 February 1991.
Press Office, German Embassy, London, telephone conversation with Peter Tatchell, 5 November 1991.

6 *Homosexual Men & Women in the Armed Forces*, ILGA, 1987.

7 *Capital Gay*, 23 November 1990.

GREECE

Until 1987, the age of consent was 16 for heterosexuals and lesbians, and 17 for gay men. Since then, it has been 15 for people of all sexualities. Article 347 of the penal code does, however, include the discriminatory provision that the 'seduction' of a person aged 15 or 16 resulting in anal intercourse is an offence. What constitutes seduction is not defined in law.[1]

Under legislation passed in 1981 concerning the protection of public health, the police are empowered to require people to be tested for sexually-transmitted diseases. This law is sometimes used to harass the gay community, with the police forcing gay men to be tested against their will.[2]

Discreet male homosexuality is quite prevalent, though public disapproval and periodic police repression results in few openly homosexual people and a low-profile lesbian and gay community.

In 1991, the editor of the Greek lesbian and gay magazine, *Amphi*, was sentenced to five months gaol and fined 50,000 drachmas for publishing 'indecent' materials. The sentence arose from *Amphi*'s publication of a statement requesting heterosexual men to stop replying to the magazine's lesbian personal ads. This request was deemed to have maligned Greek manhood and was declared 'indecent and offensive to public feeling', contrary to Paragraphs 29-31 of Clause 5060/31 of the penal code.[3]

1 Press Office, Greek Embassy, London, March 1990.
Iceberg Report, Utrecht University, 1990, p. 20.

2   Ibid., p. 48.
3   *Capital Gay,* 29 November 1991.

HUNGARY

The anti-gay and anti-lesbian proscriptions were repealed in 1961. Homosexuality was then made legal for men and women from the age of 20 years. In 1978, the minimum age was lowered to 18. This remains considerably higher than the age of consent of 14 which exists for heterosexuals. Homosexuality also still continues to be referred to in the pejorative language of 'illicit sexual practices' in Section 199 of the penal code.[1]

Nevertheless, lesbian and gay issues are increasingly and more positively discussed in plays, books, films and newspapers.

This change in attitudes began under the Communist regime and was largely prompted by the formation in 1988 of the homosexual rights organization Homeros Lambda. It's inaugural meeting was attended by representatives from the then Hungarian Communist government.

Homeros Lambda was the first officially approved lesbian and gay organization in Eastern Europe and the first autonomous social movement in Hungary to get recognition from the Communist authorities. Since democratization, co-operation has continued with the new government, particularly around the issue of HIV education and prevention.

Despite steadily more liberal attitudes towards homosexuality, Homeros Lambda has faced periodic police harassment and gay-bashing attacks at its headquarters in Budapest.

1   *Homosexualität im Europa*, Hosi Wien, 1989, p. 5-7.

ICELAND

Prior to 1940, there was no mention of homosexuality in the penal code. Though technically not illegal, gay sexuality was nevertheless heavily repressed. Since 1940, the age of consent for gay men has been 18. For heterosexuals and lesbians it is 16. While heterosexual prostitution is legal, homosexual prostitution is not.[1]

In 1991, the government agreed to set up a parliamentary commission to examine proposals to remove all distinctions between heterosexuality and homosexuality from the penal code. Proposals along these lines are likely to become law by the mid-1990s.[2]

For a long time, Iceland was the least progressive Nordic country with regard to lesbian and gay rights. This led many homosexuals to emigrate to Sweden, Norway and Denmark. In recent years, however, attitudes have begun to change. The lesbian and gay movement Samtokin 78 receives financial support from the government. An out lesbian candidate stood in the last general election. Icelandic radio now broadcasts news and personal messages for lesbian and gay listeners.[3]

1   Press Office, Icelandic Embassy, London, March 1990.
    Homosexualität im Europa, Hosi Wien, 1989, p. 5.
2   *The Pink Paper*, 5 October 1991.
3   Ibid.

IRELAND

The age of consent for heterosexuals, and for lesbians by default, is 17. However, under the Offences Against the Persons Act of 1861, and the Criminal Law Amendment Act of 1885, all sexual acts between men remain completely illegal. The 1861 law against the 'abominable crime of buggery' was originally introduced during the period of British colonial administration. It provides for a maximum sentence of life imprisonment with hard labour. Even mere attempted homosexuality carries a penalty of up to ten years gaol. In recent years, however, these laws have been rarely enforced.[1]

In 1988, the openly gay Irish senator David Norris won his appeal against the anti-gay laws in the European Court of Human Rights. The Court ordered the Irish government to decriminalize homosexuality and Ministers have indicated that they will do so — though three years after the European Court's decision they have still not introduced decriminalization legislation.

Paradoxically, though gayness remains unlawful, in November 1989 the Irish parliament overwhelmingly agreed the Prohibition of Incitement to Hatred Act. This makes it illegal to incite hatred on account of a person's 'race, colour, nationality, religion, ethnic or national origins, membership of the travelling community, or sexual orientation'.[2]

In 1990, the Irish Law Reform Commission recommended a common age of consent of 15 for same-sex and opposite-sex behaviour, except for anal intercourse where it suggested an age of consent of 17 for the penetrated partner.

Until 1973, homosexuals were forbidden to enlist in the armed forces according to Article 12 of the Defence Forces Regulations. Since then, in theory, homosexuals who are celibate can belong to the military. In practice, they tend to be discharged if their gayness is revealed.[3]

According to government guidelines it is illegal in the civil service to discriminate on account of a person's sexuality or HIV status.[4]

This commitment to oppose discrimination does not, however, apply to the availability of lesbian and gay literature. In October 1990, a gay book for children, *Jenny Lives with Eric & Martin*, was banned as 'indecent or obscene' by the Censorship of Publications Board — even though it contains nothing pornographic and is merely about the everyday life of a young girl who lives with her father and his male lover.

1   *Second ILGA Pink Book*, Utrecht University, 1988, p. 234.
2   *Capital Gay*, 15 December 1989.
3   *Capital Gay*, 18 May 1990.
4   *Homosexual Men & Women in the Armed Forces*, ILGA, 1987.
5   *Iceberg Report*, Utrecht University, 1990, p. 38.

ITALY

Though homosexual acts between men were first made lawful in some of the Italian principalities in 1792, they were not decriminalized throughout the whole country by the unified Italian state until 1889. In that year, a common age of consent of 14 was introduced for people of all sexualities, with the caveat that sex with 14 and 15 year olds can be punishable if the younger person is 'sexually innocent' and 'morally pure' and if they make a complaint to the authorities.[1]

Despite more than a century of official legalization, the public decency laws are still used against homosexual behaviour. In 1982, two men were imprisoned for kissing in the street in the Sicilian town Agrigento.

There is no explicit legal recognition of lesbian and gay partnerships. However, in an attempt to give legal recognition to unmarried heterosexual couples, the Italian government also inadvertently opened the door to the *de facto* legal recognition of lesbian and gay couples when it issued new regulations for municipal registration and record offices in 1989. These define a family as 'a group of cohabiting persons tied by bonds of affection', without specifying that the partners have to be of the opposite sex. This *de facto* recognition of same-sex relationships does not, however, give the couples concerned any legal rights.[2]

1   *Homosexualität im Europa*, Hosi Wien, 1989, p. 6-8.
2   *The Guardian*, 5 August 1989.

LATVIA

The annexation of Latvia by the Soviet Union in 1940 resulted in the imposition of the Soviet proscriptions against anal sex between men. Article 124 of the criminal code stipulates five years imprisonment for violations. In 1991, the Latvian parliament voted, in principle, to repeal Article 124; thereby paving the way for the establishment of an equal age of consent of 16 for both heterosexuals and homosexuals in the near future.[1]

This parliamentary vote followed lobbying by the country's first lesbian and gay organization, the Latvian Association for Sexual Equality, which was founded in November 1990. The organization's campaigning priorities are the decriminalization of sex between men, anti-discrimination legislation, and improved public education to stop the spread of HIV.[2]

1   *Gay Times*, August 1991.
2   *Gay Times*, May 1991.

LITHUANIA

Homosexual intercourse is still a criminal offence in all circumstances, according to Article 122 of the Soviet-inspired penal code. It is punishable by up to five years hard labour; though prosecutions are rare. In contrast, the age of consent for sex between men and women is 16. Lesbianism has never been illegal and the *de facto* age of consent for female homosexual sex is thus the same as for heterosexual women.

Following its declaration of independence, Lithuania is in the process of revising its legal system. This could result in the scrapping of anti-gay laws in the next couple of years. However, public attitudes to homosexuality remain problematic. A poll in 1991 found that 71 per cent of Lithuanians were opposed to lesbians and gay men being allowed to teach in schools, and 52 per cent thought that Aids might be divine punishment for immoral behaviour.[1]

1   *The Guardian*, 4 October 1991.

LUXEMBURG

Sex between men was legalized in 1792. No age of consent existed until 1854 when 14 years became the legal minimum for both heterosexuals and homosexuals. In 1971, while the heterosexual age of consent remained at 14, a discriminatory age of 18 years was promulgated for gay men under Section 372 of the penal code. It stipulates a maximum of three years imprisonment for violations.[1]

With regard to sentences for other sexual offences, such as indecent assault, homosexuals are usually punished much more severely than heterosexuals who commit comparable crimes.

In 1984, a majority of the Committee for Legal Affairs of the Chamber of Representatives recommended that Section 372 should be abolished. Proposals to introduce an equal age of consent of 15 or 16 for everyone have been under consideration since 1990.

1   *Homosexualität im Europa*, Hosi Wien, 1989, p. 5-7.
    Second ILGA Pink Book, Utrecht University, 1988, p. 235.

MALTA

Homosexuality has never been specifically mentioned in criminal law. However, anal sex was deemed to be an offence under the legislation against 'unnatural carnal connection' (Section 220 of the criminal code). This was repealed in 1973. Today, there is no explicit age of consent for either heterosexuals or homosexuals. Nevertheless, in practice, the age of majority (18) is treated as the age of consent. It is applied to everyone equally. According to Section 203 of the criminal code, age of consent violations involving persons aged 12-17 are only prosecuted in cases where the younger person files a complaint. The exception is cases where there is 'abuse of parental authority or of tutorship' by an adult. If these involve a person under the age of 18, the adult is prosecuted irrespective of whether there is a complaint.[1]

The population is 95 per cent Catholic, which tends to encourage homophobia. Though there are gay bars, the lesbian and gay community is unorganized and barely visible.

1   Office of the Attorney General, Valletta, Malta, fax to Peter Tatchell dated 12 December 1991.
Press Office, Maltese High Commission, London, letter to the Stonewall Group dated 3 July 1991.

NETHERLANDS

The total ban on male homosexuality was lifted in 1811. For 100 years there was no age of consent. In 1911, the minimum age was set at 18 for heterosexuals and 21 for gay men. This discriminatory legislation was repealed in 1971 when a uniform age of consent of 16 was enacted for heterosexuals, lesbians and gay men. Today, the penal code does not distinguish in any way between heterosexual and homosexual acts.[1]

In 1990, the Netherlands amended its age of consent laws. Sexual contact with 12-15 year olds is now only prosecuted in cases where there is a formal complaint.[2]

Lesbians and gay men are protected against homophobic discrimination. According to Article 1 of the Dutch constitution: 'Discrimination on the grounds of religion, belief, political opinion, race or sex, or any grounds whatsoever, shall not be permitted'. The words 'on any grounds whatsoever' have been upheld by parliament and the courts as prohibiting discrimination on the basis of sexual orientation. Nevertheless, the Dutch government is now looking at proposals for explicit anti-discrimination laws to give lesbians and gay men swift and comprehensive legal redress against the denial of equal opportunities.

While the legal system doesn't give specific recognition to same-sex partnerships, homosexual couples can draw up a legal contract which gives them many of the rights enjoyed by married heterosexual people. It can cover things like the inheritance of property and next-of-kin visiting rights in hospitals and prisons. In addition, some employers grant the partners of homosexual employees who have drawn up such contracts the same corporate perks that are available to the husbands and wives of heterosexual employees.[3]

In February 1990, the Amsterdam District Court ruled that although the present laws of the Netherlands do not specify that marriage partners must be of different sexes, this was the intention of the legislators. Hearing a case brought by two gay men against the refusal of the Amsterdam registry office to marry them, Mr Justice Schroeder said it was up to the politicians, rather than the courts, to decide on such matters.[4]

In a subsequent case, in October 1990, involving a lesbian couple who were refused the right to marry in Rotterdam, the Dutch Supreme Court dismissed their appeal, but admitted that it was not necessarily reasonable or justifiable for same-sex partners to be denied the legal rights accorded to married heterosexual couples.[5]

This legal impasse was partially broken following the decision of the municipal authorities in the town of Deventer to recognize lesbian and gay partnerships. As a result, at the City Hall in June 1991, a lesbian couple became the first same-sex partners in the Netherlands to have their relationship officially recognized in a civil marriage ceremony.[6] By November 1991, fourteen other towns had followed suit and sanctioned same-sex marriages.

Proposals to give legal recognition to lesbian and gay relationships have now been accepted by all the Dutch political parties, except the small right-wing VVD.

The Dutch Council for Youth Policy published a report in 1990 calling for same-sex couples to be given the right to adopt children (it's currently only discretionary). A majority of Dutch MPs back the proposal, but it's being vetoed by the right-wing Christian Democrat government.

Since 1974, gayness among military personnel has not been a bar to membership of the armed forces.[7] Indeed, the Dutch lesbian and gay movement has a working group consisting of serving homosexual personnel which liaises with the Ministry of Defence on issues of concern to homosexual members of the military.

Foreign partners of Dutch lesbians and gay men have been permitted to immigrate and take up residence with their lovers on much the same basis as people in heterosexual relationships.

Political asylum has also been granted to homosexuals facing persecution in their country of origin; as in the case of two Romanian gay men who were given asylum in 1991.

The lesbian and gay movement in the Netherlands is the oldest in the world, existing continuously since the beginning of the century.

1   *Homosexualität im Europa*, Hosi Wien, 1989, p. 6-9.
    Capital Gay, 9 February 1990.
2   *Gay Times*, December 1990.
    The Guardian, 11 January 1991.
3   *Iceberg Report*, Utrecht University, 1990, p. 31.
4   Ibid., p. 30.
5   Ibid., p. 30.
6   *Gay Times*, August 1991.
7   *Homosexual Men & Women in the Armed Forces*, ILGA, 1987.

NORWAY

Until 1972, all male homosexual acts were against the law. Since then, the age of consent has been 16 for everyone without distinction.[1]

In 1981, discrimination and inciting hatred against lesbians and gay men was banned. Section 349a of the penal code states that it is an offence to 'refuse a person or group of persons the sale of goods or the provision of facilities on the grounds of homosexual orientation or way of life'. The maximum penalty is six months gaol. Under Section 135a, it is unlawful to 'publicly threaten, insult or bear hatred towards, persecute or hold in contempt, a person or group on the grounds of homosexual orientation or way of life'. Breaches are punishable by up to two years in gaol. An Evangelical church minister was convicted under this law for anti-homosexual remarks on the radio and was fined 2,500 Norwegian crowns.[2]

Homosexuals are free to enlist in the armed forces, and practising homosexuality by service personnel is not a disciplinary offence.[3] New recruits are given an information brochure which states that 'lesbians and gays are an important minority in Norway's army', and it lists details of lesbian and gay organizations, including those which exist within the military for homosexual personnel.[4]

At the discretion of the authorities, the overseas partners of Norwegian lesbians and gay men can get residence rights and work permits on proof of a committed, long term relationship.[5]

Asylum has been granted to foreign homosexuals on humanitarian grounds. It has been made available to Iranians and Chileans whose homosexuality put them at risk of repression if they had been required to return to their country of birth. In one case, asylum was also granted to a Moroccan-Israeli gay couple who argued that they were effectively stateless since neither of their home countries would accept their partner for immigration and residence.

In 1990, the Norwegian lesbian and gay movement received a government grant equivalent to £110,000.

Over the last decade, opinion polls have consistently shown that around 80 per cent of Norwegians favour equal rights for lesbians and gay men.

1   *Homosexualität im Europa*, Hosi Wien, 1989, p. 6.
2   *Second ILGA Pink Book*, Utrecht University, 1988, p. 238.
3   *Homosexual Men & Women in the Armed Forces*, ILGA, 1987.
4   *The Pink Paper*, 23 November 1991.
5   *Iceberg Report*, Utrecht University, 1990, p. 32.

POLAND

In 1932, Poland decriminalized male homosexuality and instituted an equal age of consent of 15 for heterosexuals, lesbians and gay men. The laws against gay prostitution were rescinded in 1969.[1]

However, despite these reforms, as recently as 1988 there were violent police raids on gay cafes, and some local police forces admitted keeping special files on known homosexuals.[2] In the days of the old Communist regime, these were sometimes used by the police to blackmail lesbians and gay men into acting as informers.

The first lesbian and gay organization, ETAP, was founded in the city of Wroclaw in 1986, followed by Filo in Gdansk and the Warsaw Homosexual Movement in the capital. In 1988, the WHM applied for official government recognition. Its application was supported by 14 leading public figures, including Professor Kozakiewicz, the then head of the Association for Family Protection who, in 1990, was elected an MP and became the Speaker of the Solidarity-led Polish parliament.

In recent years, lesbianism and gayness have been discussed fairly positively in all sections of the media. Influenced by the ideas of progressive academics such as Professor Boczkowski, same-sex relations are being increasingly portrayed by the press as one variation among many and as being equally valid as heterosexuality. Gay personal ads, along the lines of 'girl seeks girlfriend', now appear in many newspapers. Reporting about Aids has also generally been objective and has avoided scapegoating the homosexual community.

There are lesbian and gay organizations in most major cities and six regular homosexual magazines. In October 1989, these organizations and magazines joined together to form the Lambda Groups Association of Poland, which won official legal recognition in March 1990.

1 *Homosexualität im Europa*, Hosi Wien, 1989, p. 6-8.
2 *The Pink Paper*, 10 February 1990.

PORTUGAL

The ban on sex between men was ended in 1852. Under the criminal code legislated in 1982, the age of consent is 16 for all.[1] Furthermore, sexual relations with 12-15 year olds are usually only prosecuted if the younger person is deceived or pressured into sex, and if they subsequently make a complaint. However, all sexual behaviour with young people under 12 is automatically punishable by a prison sentence of two to eight years.[2]

The one homophobic element in the criminal code is Article 207 — 'Homosexuality with Minors'. It stipulates up to three years gaol for anyone over the age of majority (18) who has sex with a person of the same sex under 16 contrary to *pudor* (the accepted standards of sexual morality). There is no Article in the criminal code which penalizes comparable heterosexual behaviour.[3]

In addition, Article 22 of the Law on Military Service excludes from the armed forces those who have been involved in 'offensive acts'. This Article has, in the past, been interpreted to exclude homosexuals.

The courts have also occasionally denied lesbian and gay parents access to and custody of their children following divorce.

1 *Homosexualität im Europa*, Hosi Wien, 1989, p. 6-8.
2 Press Office, Portuguese Embassy, London, fax to Peter Tatchell, 6 November 1991.
3 Ibid.

ROMANIA

All lesbian and gay behaviour is illegal under Article 200 of the penal code which specifies a sentence of up to five years for offenders. Under Article 204, even attempted homosexual sex is severely punishable. For heterosexuals, the age of consent is 14 years.[1]

Romania is the most homophobic country in Europe. Homosexuality is regarded as a sickness. According to one gay man who smuggled a letter to the Austrian lesbian and gay movement, Hosi Wien: 'Romania is still in the Middle Ages.

Homosexuality is considered an illness. Psychiatric treatment is employed with the intention of "curing" or "normalizing" us'. Indeed, lesbians and gay men have been incarcerated in psychiatric hospitals and forcibly treated with drugs, electric-shock therapy and even castration to 'cure' their 'sexual perversion'.[2]

Accusations of homosexuality were frequently used by the Communist regime of Nicolae Ceausescu to discredit political dissidents. During his rule, the police kept extensive files on all known or suspected homosexuals (they probably still do). These were maintained and expanded by interrogation and torture, and by the blackmail of gay men to get them to inform on others. Being an unmarried adult often led to suspicion of homosexuality and police surveillance.[3]

In 1987, there were large-scale arrests of gay men. Many were tortured. At least one committed suicide by jumping from a police station window. Prominent victims of the anti-gay witch-hunts over the last decade have included Émile Riman, the former head of the Bucharest State Opera; Gabriel Popescu, one of the country's foremost dancers; and Crin Teodorescu, the theatre director who was driven to take his own life.[4]

There has been no change in the law since the overthrow of the Ceausescu regime in December 1989. However, a spin-off effect of the now generally more liberal atmosphere has been an easing of the police harassment of gay people and the first signs of homosexual visibility in bars and cruising areas. In 1991, a Romanian newspaper published an article *Lesbians out of the Shadows* and a gay group began to meet at Bucharest University. With the preparation of a new democratic constitution and penal code under way, it is possible that homosexuality may be decriminalized in the not too distant future.

1   *Second ILGA Pink Book*, Utrecht University, 1988, p. 239.
2   *Report of the Eastern European Information Pool*, Hosi Wien, June 1985, p. 11-14.
    Capital Gay, 12 January 1990.
    The Pink Paper, 3 February 1990.
    Gay Times, March 1990.
3   Ibid.
4   Ibid.

ex-SOVIET REPUBLICS

Soon after the 1917 Bolshevik Revolution, all the old Tsarist laws were abolished, including those criminalizing homosexual relations. The new Soviet criminal codes of 1922 and 1926 didn't mention homosexuality at all.

In 1934, however, Stalin recriminalized gay male sex and ordered large-scale purges of homosexuals. Thousands were dismissed from the Communist Party, the government, and the armed forces. Many were imprisoned as 'Fascist agents' and 'bourgeois deviationists'.

Stalin's legal proscriptions remain in force today. Article 121 of the Russian penal code, for example, states that anal intercourse between men is a criminal offence punishable by up to five years hard labour. It is estimated that about 800 men a year are arrested for violations of Article 121 (often as a result of sexually-transmitted disease clinics informing on gay patients).[1] However, in practice all gay and bisexual men risk harassment for any form of same-sex behaviour. The age of consent for heterosexual — and by default lesbian — behaviour is 16. In theory, homosexual acts other than sodomy, such as oral sex and mutual masturbation, are lawful.

In 1987, government officials and lawyers gave assurances that the anti-gay laws would not be included in the new Soviet penal code, which was then in the process of being drafted. However, by 1989, these same people were expressing anxiety that, with little public understanding or tolerance of homosexuality, this reform could generate a homophobic backlash which might be exploited by conservative Communist factions, and by right-wing nationalist groups like Pamyat, in order to destabilize the democratization process. By 1991, there were indications that the Soviet government was back-tracking on its earlier pledge to legalize gay sex. This followed evidence that the Soviet public is deeply hostile to decriminalization, with 35 per cent of respondents in a 1991 opinion poll saying that all homosexuals should be executed.[2]

Prior to the reformist Gorbachev era, these prejudiced attitudes were given free rein by the Soviet state. In the 1970s, the film director Sergei Paradzhanov and the poet Gennady Trifonov were among those imprisoned for their homosexuality.

Both were sentenced to several years hard labour. During the same period, lesbians and gay men were often blackmailed into working for the KGB (as an alternative to imprisonment). Aversion therapy was a common 'treatment' for homosexuality.

Since the mid-1980s, however, the new atmosphere of *glasnost* has led to a gradual liberalization of official attitudes. The Young Communist League's daily newspaper, *Komsolmolskaya Pravda*, began carrying articles and letters about lesbian and gay issues in 1986. Other state-run newspapers quickly followed suit, with mainly positive coverage. In 1989, the first gay personal ads appeared in the Soviet press.

Bars and cruising areas frequented by homosexuals have been left largely unmolested by the authorities in recent years. Notable exceptions were the violent police raids in 1990 on bars popular with gay men in the Black Sea resort of Sochi.

1990 was a watershed year in the struggle for lesbian and gay equality in the USSR. The country's first homosexual rights movements were publicly launched early that year — the Moscow Union of Lesbians and Gay Men (MULGM) and the Tchaikovsky Foundation in St Petersburg (formerly Leningrad). The first ever conference on the politics, culture and history of homosexuality — 'Sexual Minorities & Society: Changing Attitudes Towards Homosexuality' — took place in the Estonian capital of Tallinn in May. Two months later, MULGM members were savagely clubbed by police officers when they picketed the 28th Congress of the Soviet Communist Party in the Kremlin to demand the repeal of Article 121 and tougher government action against Aids.

In mid-1991, the Soviet Union's first Lesbian and Gay Pride Festival took place in St Petersburg and Moscow. The two week event, which included a conference and film festival, was attended by a total of nearly 20,000 people. The highlights were a gay rights demonstration outside the Bolshoi Theatre and an impromptu 'kiss-in' in a Moscow street.

Despite greater official openness about lesbian and gay issues, the traditional homophobia of the Soviet state continues to resurface from time to time. A gay man arrested in a police raid on an unofficial gay bar in Moscow in 1988 was pressured to become an informer. When he refused, the police threatened his life and informed the Communist youth organization that he was homosexual. They had him forcibly committed to a mental institution, where he was held in solitary confinement and given coma-inducing drugs.[3]

In 1991, the Vice Department of the Soviet Militia in Moscow admitted that, as part of a campaign to monitor and control the spread of HIV, it holds files on thousands of gay men and keeps homosexual meeting places under surveillance.[4]

There have also been a series of sustained attacks on the fledgeling lesbian and gay rights movement. The KGB is widely suspected as having been behind the ransacking in 1990 of the offices of the MULGM newspaper, *Tema*, and the theft of its documents, address lists and publishing materials.[5] Around the same time, in an apparent attempt to discredit MULGM and *Tema*, the official Soviet press, including *Pravda*, mounted a vicious smear campaign which falsely accused them of promoting paedophilia, child prostitution and necrophilia.[6] Also in 1990, the police charged the St Petersburg lesbian activist Olga Zhuk with the offences of 'gathering groups of criminals' and violating Article 121 (the anti-sodomy law which criminalizes anal sex between men!).[7] Faced with these attacks by the Soviet authorities, the lesbian and gay movement has received the backing of the radical St Petersburg and Moscow City Councils and the popular liberal newspaper, *Ogonyok*.

In September 1991, coinciding with a Moscow meeting of the Conference on Security and Co-operation in Europe, the Soviet lesbian and gay movement hosted a parallel homosexual human rights conference. It submitted a declaration to the CSCE urging the member states to 'take measures to eliminate and prevent discrimination against persons based on their sexual orientation'. The conference also called on presidents Gorbachev and Yeltsin to repeal the anti-sodomy laws and to free all lesbians and gay men held in prisons and psychiatric hospitals because of their homosexuality or their political activity in support of homosexual equality.[8]

The break up of the centralized Soviet Union and the creation of the newly-independent republics, will probably hasten the further decriminalization of homosexuality in the westernized states such as Latvia, Estonia and Lithuania (already in late 1991, the Ukraine became the first ex-Soviet republic to repeal its ban on sodomy). The dissolution of the USSR may, however, set back the struggle for lesbian and gay equality in the Muslim-dominated republics and those where conservative nationalists have won power.

1   *The Pink Paper*, 17 March 1990.
    Capital Gay, 23 November 1990.
2   *News at Ten*, ITN, London, 28 August 1991.
3   *Gay Times*, January 1991.
4   *Gay Times*, August 1991.
5   *Capital Gay*, 5 October 1990.
6   *Capital Gay*, 29 March 1991.
7   *Capital Gay*, 21 December 1990.
8   *Gay Times*, October 1991.

SPAIN

Male homosexual acts were first legalized in 1822. They were made lawful from the age of 12 — the same age as for heterosexuals. However, since then, homosexuality has twice been heavily repressed: during the military dictatorship of General Primo de Rivera from 1923-30 and during the regime of General Franco between 1939-75. Under Franco, the harsh public morality laws were often used against gay men and an age of consent of 23 was enforced. These laws were repealed in 1978. Today, the age of consent is once again 12 for heterosexuals and homosexuals alike. Sexual relations with people aged between 12 and 18 can only be prosecuted if the younger person is deceived or if an older person abuses a position of authority. Even then, charges are only laid if someone makes a complaint.[1]

Despite these liberal laws, there are still vestiges of public intolerance and police harassment. In 1986, two lesbians caught kissing in a Madrid street were arrested and detained by the police for 42 hours before being released without charge.

Since 1984, it has been legal for homosexuals to belong to the armed forces, providing sexual contacts do not take place in barracks or during duty hours.[2]

In 1983, the congress of the governing Socialist Party urged action against homophobic discrimination. The government responded by establishing a unit responsible for lesbian and gay issues within the Department of Social Affairs. Two years later, the Spanish parliament endorsed Recommendation 924 and Resolution 756 of the Council of Europe, condemning anti-homosexual discrimination and calling for lesbians and gay men to be accorded equal rights in law.[3]

The absence of legal status for lesbian and gay partnerships was confirmed in 1987 when the courts upheld the decision of a Catalan registry office which had refused to marry two men. This prompted the Attorney-General of Catalonia to publicly speak out in support of law reform. He said that partners of the same sex should have the right to be legally recognized as a couple.[4]

1 *Homosexualität im Europa*, Hosi Wien, 1989, p. 6-9.
   Independent on Sunday, 29 September 1991.
2 *Homosexual Men & Women in the Armed Forces*, ILGA, 1987.
3 *Iceberg Report*, Utrecht University, 1990, p. 11-12.
4 Ibid., p. 31.

SWEDEN

Until 1944, both lesbianism and gayness were against the law. In that year, homosexual acts were decriminalized. Subsequent reforms eventually led to the introduction of a common age of consent of 15 years in 1978.[1] However, if a young person is in the official care of someone holding a position of authority, such as a teacher or a social worker, the age of consent is 18 (this applies to both heterosexual and homosexual relationships). The maximum penalty for violations of the age of consent is eight years imprisonment.[2]

Since 1979, homosexuality has no longer been officially classified as a disease.

Protection against discrimination was enacted in a 1987 law which forbids public officials and private businesses to discriminate in the provision of goods and services on the basis of homosexual orientation. However, despite this law, insemination by donor is restricted to women who are married or cohabiting with a man, and is therefore not available to lesbians.[3]

Also in 1987, the Homosexual Co-Habitees Act gave legal recognition to lesbian and gay relationships and granted homosexual couples equal rights with heterosexual co-habitees with regard to inheritance, property rights and taxation. A parliamentary commission was set up in 1991 to study proposals for Danish-style same-sex partnership laws.

Homosexuals have a wide range of other social rights: lesbian and gay individuals (but not couples) are allowed to foster and adopt children; active homosexuals are free to serve in the military; government guidelines on sex education lessons in schools encourage the presentation of homosexuality as a valid and positive lifestyle; foreign lesbians and gay men cohabiting in committed relationships with Swedish citizens are allowed permanent residency; and political asylum has been granted to homosexuals fleeing repression abroad.[4]

Indeed, under Article 31 of the Aliens Regulations, the Swedish immigration department has officially ruled that a homosexual person can be granted asylum on 'humanitarian' grounds if they are in danger of persecution because of their sexual orientation in their home country. However, what constitutes a danger of persecution is open to interpretation. A gay Soviet refugee was refused asylum in 1991 because the threat of victimization in the USSR was not deemed to be serious enough (though he was eventually given a residence permit on a legal technicality).[5] In another asylum case, two gay partners, one British and the other Malaysian, were allowed to stay in Sweden because neither of their home countries would accept the other partner for residence.

In 1990, the government's annual grant to 12 lesbian and gay organizations amounted to £100,000.

1   *Homosexualität im Europa*, Hosi Wien, 1989, p. 6.
2   Press Office, Swedish Embassy, London, fax to Peter Tatchell dated 30 January 1990.
3   Ibid.
4   Ibid.
5   *Gay Times,* May 1991.

SWITZERLAND

Gay sex was progressively legalized in each of the Swiss cantons between 1937 and 1942. The age of consent was set at 16 years, the same as for heterosexuals. However, there was a discriminatory qualification for gay and bisexual men: it was an offence to 'seduce' a young man between the ages of 16 and 20. Seduction was not defined in law. It was often interpreted by the courts to criminalize all homosexual relations with 16-20-year-old men.[1]

In 1991, this discriminatory clause concerning homosexual 'seduction' was repealed, together with the discriminatory restrictions on homosexual prostitution and on homosexual relations by serving members of the armed forces.[2] A new law, introduced the same year, decriminalized consenting hetero and homo sex involving youths under 16, providing there is no more than three years difference in the partners' ages.[3]

Despite formal legal equality, it was revealed in 1990 that the police in the Swiss capital of Berne kept extensive records on gay men, including intimate details about their sexual habits.

Also in 1990, following controversy over the queer-bashing of two gay couples who were kissing in a Berne swimming pool, the Town Tribunal ruled that same-sex partners should be allowed to kiss in municipal facilities.

1   *Iceberg Report*, Utrecht University, 1990, p. 21
    Homosexualität im Europa, Hosi Wien, 1989, p. 6-9.
2   *Gay Times*, April 1991.
3   *Capital Gay*, 23 August, 1990.

TURKEY

Homosexuality has never been totally banned in modern times and the wording of the current law does not discriminate. The minimum age for vaginal and anal intercourse is 18. Other sexual acts are lawful for both heterosexuals and homosexuals from the age of 15.[1] Despite these non-discriminatory legal statutes, there is a high level of public intolerance and state repression against the lesbian and gay community.

In response to a very macho heterosexual society, male homosexuality in Turkey is often expressed in the form of gay

transvestitism. Paradoxically, gay transvestites are publicly re-
viled but privately prized as exotic sexual partners by ostensibly
heterosexual men. This tends to encourage gay transvestitism
and prostitution, which intensifies the police repression of the
homosexual community.

According to the law, a person can be rounded up at the
discretion of the police, without warrant, and forcibly taken to
a sexually-transmitted diseases clinic for compulsory testing.
This law is often used to harass homosexuals.[2]

In 1986, the police raided gay bars throughout Istanbul,
beating gay men and dragging them out into the street. Many
were tortured, had their heads shaven, and were tested against
their will for venereal diseases. In protest, lesbian and gay
activists staged a series of hunger strikes.[3]

In 1989, the publishers of *Yesil Baris*, the newspaper of the
Turkish Radical Green Party, were charged with 'spreading
homosexual information' and 'slandering the state' following
their publication of a series of articles about lesbian and gay
issues, including the suggestion that the founder of modern
Turkey, Kemal Ataturk, was a homosexual.[4]

One of the party's top leaders, Ibrahim Eren, who is also the
country's best known gay activist, was arrested in December
1989 after he held a press conference where he condemned
violent police raids against the gay transvestite communities.
These raids resulted in two men committing suicide, one of
whom was a 17-year-old youth who threw himself from the top
of a six-floor building. Eren was detained for three months in
Bayrampasa Prison on charges of violating the regulations
against unlawful public assemblies.[5]

In 1990, Eren was arrested again. Badly beaten by the police,
he suffered a perforated ear drum and three broken ribs. Falsely
charged with promoting homosexual prostitution at his sauna
business in Istanbul, Eren was imprisoned for a further two
weeks in Sagmalcular Prison.[6]

A survey of 223 Turkish gay men by Arzlan Yuzgun in 1986
revealed that 96.4 per cent complained about police victimization: 61 per cent had been abused or humiliated by the police;
41.3 per cent had been arrested and taken to a police station; and
13.5 per cent had had their heads shaved by the police. A further

31.4 per cent had experienced being forcibly sent to a VD clinic.[7]

In the continuing saga of state repression, at least 40 gay transvestites in the Cihangir district of Istanbul were stripped and beaten by police wielding plastic hose-pipes in May 1991.[8]

1   *Homosexualität im Europa*, Hosi Wien, 1989, p. 6-9.
    Press Office, Turkish Embassy, London, letter to Peter Tatchell dated 16 February 1990.
2   *Second ILGA Pink Book*, Utrecht University, 1988, p. 155.
3   *Capital Gay*, 9 June, 1989.
4   Ibid.
5   *Capital Gay*, 9 February 1990.
    Capital Gay, 26 July 1991.
6   *Gay Times*, August 1990.
7   *Second ILGA Pink Book*, Utrecht University, 1988, p. 155.
8   *Capital Gay*, 17 May 1991.

ex-YUGOSLAV REPUBLICS

Before 1977, homosexual acts between men were illegal throughout all of Yugoslavia. In that year, power was devolved to the six constituent republics. Slovenia and Montenegro legalized gay male sex with an age of consent equal to that of heterosexuals (14). The republic of Croatia also decriminalized homosexuality in 1977 but brought in a discriminatory age of consent of 18 years, compared with 14 for heterosexuals.[1] In the republics of Bosnia-Herzegovina, Macedonia and Serbia, the total ban on same sex relationships was maintained. The maximum sentence for violations in these latter three republics is one year gaol; though there is no record of any convictions over the last decade.[2]

So far as child custody for lesbian and gay parents is concerned: 'The courts usually evaluate homosexuality as a specific negative circumstance which may negatively affect the psychophysical development of the child', according to Jovan Ciric, the director of the Institute of Criminological and Sociological Research in Belgrade.[3]

A similar repressive attitude prevails with regard to homosexuals serving in the armed forces. Ciric says: 'There is a practice in the Army that homosexual soldiers be declared unable to serve their term in the military...due to their homosexual abnormality'.[4]

Ignorance about homosexuality and related issues is still considerable. A lesbian and gay rights conference scheduled to take place in the city of Ljubljana in 1987 was cancelled by the local health authorities because they feared it would encourage the spread of HIV. The Belgrade-based homosexual rights organization, Arkadia, was refused state registration in 1991; thereby denying it the legal right to hold public meetings.

Despite this prejudice, there have been open lesbian and gay organizations, festivals and publications in Yugoslavia since 1984: The gay magazine *Revolver* is published with the aid of a grant from Ljubljana city council, and a weekly gay radio programme is broadcast by Belgrade's independent station, B92.

In 1991, the republics of Slovenia and Croatia declared independence. The draft constitution of Slovenia included an explicit commitment to equal rights for lesbians and gay men. At the time Article 7 read: 'Everybody has the same rights, regardless of nationality, race, sex, sexual orientation, language, religion, political or other opinion, or any other personal condition. All are equal before the law'.[5] However, the final version deleted the reference to 'sexual orientation' and merely refers to outlawing discrimination on the grounds of 'other personal circumstances', which may or may not be interpreted as covering homosexuality.

1   *Homosexualität im Europa*, Hosi Wien, 1989, p. 5-7 (and subsequent research by Kurt Krickler of Hosi Wien).
    Director, Institute of Criminological and Sociological Research, Belgrade, Yugoslavia, letter to Peter Tatchell, March 1990.

2   Ibid.

3   Ibid.

4   Ibid.

5   *Gay Times*, December 1990.

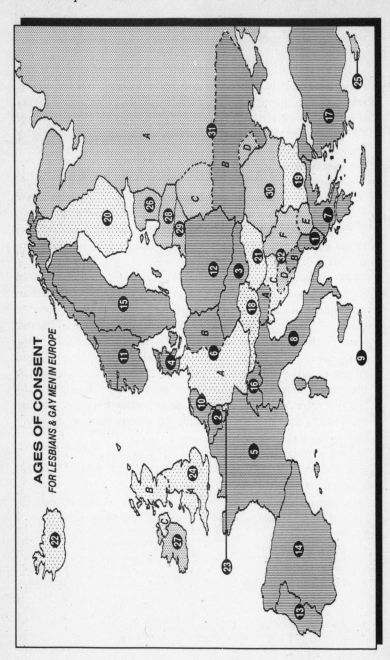

AGES OF CONSENT
FOR LESBIANS & GAY MEN IN EUROPE

Equal Ages Of Consent

1 Albania — HLG=14, 1977*
2 Belgium — HLG=16, 1792*
3 Czechoslovakia — HLG=15, 1961**
4 Denmark — HLG=15, 1930*
5 France — HLG=15,1791*
6 *B.* Germany (east) — HLG=14, 1968*
7 Greece — HLG=15, °
8 Italy — HLG=14, 1889*
9 Malta — HLG=18, 1973*
10 Netherlands — HLG=16, 1811*
11 Norway — HLG=16, 1972*
12 Poland — HLG=15, 1932*
13 Portugal — HLG=16, 1852*
14 Spain — HLG=12, 1822*
15 Sweden — HLG=15, 1944**
16 Switzerland — HLG=16, 1942*
17 Turkey — HLG=15, +
31 *B.* Ukraine (ex-Soviet Republic) — HLG = 16, 1991*
32 *A.* Slovenia & *B.* Montenegro (ex-Yugoslav Republics) — HLG=14, 1977*

Discriminatory Ages Of Consent

6 *A.* Germany (west) — HL=14 / G=18, 1969*
18 Austria — HL=14 / G=18, 1971**
19 Bulgaria — H=14 / LG=18, 1968**
20 Finland — H=16 / LG=18, 1971**
21 Hungary — H=14 / LG=18, 1961**
22 Iceland — HL=16 / G=18, +
23 Luxemburg — HL=14 / G=18, 1792*
24 UK: *A.* England & Wales — HL=16 / G=21, 1967*
   B. Scotland — HL=16 / G=21, 1980*
   C. Northern Ireland — HL=17 / G=21, 1982*
32 *C.* Croatia (ex-Yugoslav Republic) — HL=14 / G=18, 1977*

Homosexual Acts Still Completely Illegal

25 Cyprus — Ø
26 Estonia — Ø
27 Ireland — Ø
28 Latvia — Ø
29 Lithuania — Ø
30 Romania — ØØ
31 *A.* Russia, *C.* Belarus & *D.* Moldavia (ex-Soviet Republics) — Ø
32 *D.* Bosnia-Herzegovina, *E.* Macedonia & *F.* Serbia (ex-Yugoslav Republics) — Ø

Key

HLG = same age of consent for heterosexuals, lesbians and gay men
H = age of consent for heterosexuals
L = age of consent for lesbians
G = age of consent for gay men
Ø Total ban applies to gay men only
ØØ Total ban applies to both gay men and lesbians
1791 Year of decriminalization where homosexual acts were once totally illegal
* Total ban applied to gay men only
** Total ban applied to both gay men and lesbians
+ Homosexual acts were never totally illegal
° Information not available

Estonia, Latvia, Lithuania are expected to decriminalize homosexuality soon. Ireland and Romania are considering decriminalization. Germany is pledged to introduce an equal age of consent of 16 for all in 1992-93. Iceland and Luxembourg are looking at proposals for a common age of consent.

Appendix 1

International Human Rights Declarations

There are several key international human rights agreements and declarations which include comprehensive commitments to fundamental freedoms, equal rights, and non-discrimination. Though they rarely include an explicit commitment to lesbian and gay equality, they are pledged to the principle that human rights are universal and indivisible. Furthermore, their commitment to equal rights 'for all' and 'without distinction', together with their outlawing of discrimination 'on any grounds', is all-inclusive. A liberal interpretation of these agreements and declarations could therefore argue that since they give guarantees of equality to all peoples, this implicitly includes lesbians and gay men.

Universal Declaration of Human Rights
United Nations, 10 December 1948

Article 1: 'All human beings are born free and equal in dignity and rights'.

Article 2: 'Everyone is entitled to all the rights and freedoms set forth in this Declaration, without distinction of any kind, such as race, colour, sex, language, religion, political or other opinion, national or social origin, property, birth or other status'.

Article 7: 'All are equal before the law and are entitled without any discrimination to equal protection of the law'.

Article 12: 'No one shall be subjected to an arbitrary interference with his privacy'.

European Convention on Human Rights
Council of Europe, 4 November 1950

Article 14: 'The enjoyment of the rights and freedoms set forth in this Convention shall be secured without discrimination on any ground such as sex, race, colour, language, religion, political or other opinion, national or social origin, association with a national minority, property, birth or other status'.

European Social Charter
Council Of Europe, 18 October 1961

Preamble: 'Considering that the enjoyment of social rights should be secured without discrimination on grounds of race, colour, sex, religion, political opinion, national extraction or social origin...'

International Covenant on Civil & Political Rights
United Nations, 16 December 1966

Article 26: 'All persons are equal before the law and are entitled without any discrimination to the equal protection of the law. In this respect, the law shall prohibit any discrimination and guarantee to all persons equal and effective protection against discrimination on any ground such as race, colour, sex, language, religion, political or other opinion, national or social origin, property, birth or other status'.

Helsinki Final Act
Conference on Security & Co-operation in Europe (CSCE), 1 August 1975

Section (1 (a) VII): 'The participating states will respect human rights and fundamental freedoms, including the freedom of thought, conscience, religion or belief, for all without distinction as to race, sex, language or religion. They will promote and encourage the effective use of civil, political, economic, social, cultural and other rights and freedoms, all of which derive from the inherent dignity of the human person and are essential for his free will and full development'.

Recommendation 924: On Discrimination Against Homosexuals
Council Of Europe, 1 October 1981

1. Recalling its firm commitment to the protection of human rights and to the abolition of all forms of discrimination;
2. Observing that, despite some efforts and new legislation in recent years directed towards eliminating discrimination against homosexuals, they continue to suffer from discrimination and even, at times, from oppression;
3. Believing that, in the pluralistic societies of today...practices such as the exclusion of persons on the grounds of their sexual preferences from certain jobs, the existence of acts of aggression against them or the keeping of records on those persons, are survivals of several centuries of prejudice;
4. Considering that in a few member states homosexual acts are still a criminal offence and often carry severe penalties;
5. Believing that all individuals, male or female...should enjoy the right to sexual self-determination;
6. Emphasizing, however, that the state has a responsibility in areas of public concern such as the protection of children.
7. Recommends that the Committee of Ministers:
   i. Urge those member states where homosexual acts between consenting adults are liable to criminal prosecution, to abolish those laws and practices;
   ii. Urge member states to apply the same minimum age of consent for homosexual and heterosexual acts;
   iii. Call on the governments of the member states: (a) to order the destruction of existing special records on homosexuals and to abolish the practice of keeping records on homosexuals by the police or any other authority; (b) to assure equality of treatment, no more no less, for homosexuals with regard to employment, pay and job security, particularly in the public sector; (c) to ask for the cessation of all compulsory medical

action or research designed to alter the sexual orientation of adults; (d) to ensure that custody, visiting rights and accommodation of children by their parents should not be restricted on the sole grounds of the homosexual tendencies of one of them; (e) to ask prison and other public authorities to be vigilant against the risk of rape, violence and sexual offences in prisons.

Declaration of Fundamental Rights & Freedoms
European Parliament, 12 April 1989

Article 3: '1. In the field of application of Community law,everyone shall be equal before the law.
2. Any discrimination on grounds such as race, colour, sex, language, religion, political or other opinion, national or social origin, association with a national minority, property, birth or other status shall be prohibited'.

Article 6: 1. 'Everyone shall have the right to respect and protection for their identity'.

Community Charter of the Fundamental Social Rights of Workers (Social Charter)
European Community, 9 December 1989

Preamble: 'Whereas, in order to ensure equal treatment, it is important to combat every form of discrimination, including discrimination on grounds of sex, colour, race, opinions and beliefs, and whereas, in a spirit of solidarity, it is important to combat social exclusion...'

Conference on the Human Dimension of CSCE
Conference on Security & Co-operation in Europe, 29 June 1990

Article 5.9: 'All persons are equal before the law and are entitled without any discrimination to the equal protection of the law. In this respect, the law will prohibit any discrimination and guarantee to all persons equal and effective protection against discrimination on any ground'.

Charter of Paris for a New Europe
Conference on Security & Co-operation in Europe,
21 November 1990

Human Rights, Democracy and Rule of Law: 'Human Rights and fundamental freedoms are the birthright of all human beings, are inalienable and are guaranteed by law. Their protection and promotion is the first responsibility of government...

We affirm that, without discrimination, every individual has the right to: freedom of thought, conscience and religion or belief, freedom of expression...

We express our determination to combat all forms racial and ethnic hatred, anti-semitism, xenophobia and discrimination against anyone...'

European Community
Treaty Commitments

The European Community has implicit legal powers, as set out in the Preambles and Articles of its Treaties, to ensure non-discrimination against lesbians and gay men throughout the 12 member states.

While there is nothing concrete and specific in these Treaties committing the EC to homosexual equality, there are numerous statements supporting the general principles and objectives of democratic rights, individual liberties, fundamental freedoms, equal treatment, common policies, improved living and working conditions, and freedom of movement. With a liberal reading, these broad commitments can be interpreted as legally empowering, and obliging, the EC to protect the human rights of lesbian and gay people. They can be seen as constituting a *de facto*, implicit legal authority for EC action to guarantee homosexuals equal treatment — as befits a Community pledged to uphold human rights and to create a barrier-free common market:

Treaty Establishing the European Economic Community (1957)

Preamble: 'Resolved to ensure economic and social progress of their countries by common action to eliminate the barriers which divide Europe...

Affirming as the essential objective of their efforts the constant improvement of the living and working conditions of their peoples...

Resolved by thus pooling their resources to preserve and strengthen peace and liberty...'

Single European Act (1986)

Preamble: 'Determined to work together to promote democracy on the basis of the fundamental rights...notably freedom, equality and social justice...

Aware of the responsibility incumbent on Europe...to display the principles of democracy and compliance with the law and with human rights to which they are attached...

Determined to improve the economic and social situation by extending common policies and pursuing new objectives...'

Treaty Establishing the European Economic Community
(as amended by the Single European Act)

Article 2: 'The Community shall have as its task, by establishing a common market and progressively approximating the economic policies of Member States, and to promote throughout the Community a harmonious development of economic activities, a continuous and balanced expansion, an increase in stability, an accelerating raising of the standard of living and closer relations between the States belonging to it'.

Article 3: '...(c) the abolition, as between Member States, of obstacles to freedom of movement for persons...
(f) the institution of a system ensuring that competition in the common market is not distorted...
(h) the approximation of the laws of the Member States to the extent required for the proper functioning of the common market...'

Article 48: '1. Freedom of movement for workers shall be secured within the Community by the end of the transitional period at the latest...'

Article 49: 'As soon as this Treaty comes into force, the Council shall, acting by a qualified majority on a proposal from the Commission...issue directives or make regulations setting out the measures required to bring about, by progressive stages, freedom of movement for workers...'

Article 100: 'The Council shall, acting unanimously on a proposal from the Commission, issue directives for the approximation of such provisions laid down by law, regulation or administrative action in Member States as directly affect the establishment or functioning of the common market'.

Article 100a: '1. By way of derogation from Article 100...The Council shall, acting by a qualified majority on a proposal from the Commission in co-operation with the European Parliament and after consulting the Economic and Social Committee, adopt the measures for the approximation of the provisions laid down by law, regulation or administrative action in Member States which have as their object the establishment and functioning of the internal market'.

Article 101: 'Where the Commission finds that a difference between the provisions laid down by law, regulation or administrative action in Member States is distorting the conditions of competition in the common market and that the resultant distortion needs to be eliminated, it shall consult the Member States concerned.

If such consultation does not result in an agreement eliminating the distortion in question, the Council shall, on a proposal from the Commission...issue the necessary directives. The Commission and the Council may take any other appropriate measures provided for in this Treaty'.

Article 117: 'Member States agree upon the need to promote improved working conditions and an improved standard of living for workers, so as to make possible their harmonization while the improvement is being maintained.

They believe that such a development will ensue not only from the functioning of the common market, which will favour the harmonization of social systems, but also from the procedures provided for in this Treaty and from the approximation of provisions laid down by law, regulation or administrative action'.

Article 118: 'Without prejudice to the other provisions of this Treaty and in conformity with its general objectives, the Commission shall have the task of promoting close co-operation between Member States in the social field, particularly in matters relating to:
— employment;
— labour law and working conditions...'

Article 235: 'If action by the Community should prove necessary to attain, in the course of the operation of the common market, one of the objectives of the Community and this Treaty has not provided the necessary powers, the Council shall, acting unanimously on a proposal from the Commission and after consulting the European Parliament, take the appropriate measures'.

Decisions of the European Parliament

The democratically elected European Parliament is the only European Community institution which is genuinely representative of, and accountable to, the people of the member states. On five occasions since 1984, it has voted overwhelmingly in favour of various EC actions to ensure equal rights and protection against discrimination for lesbians and gay men. The key points of those resolutions are as follows:

SQUARCIALUPI REPORT *On Sexual Discrimination at the Workplace*, 13 March 1984 (OJ No C 104, 16. 4. 1984, p. 46-48):

A. Whereas the elimination of all forms of discrimination between individuals is a prerequisite to the achievement of a more just society and of the objectives laid down in the Preamble and Article 117 of the EEC Treaty, in particular that of improving the living and working conditions of the people of Europe,

B. Whereas the Treaty or its implementing provisions directly confer on the citizens of the Community the right to move freely and to reside on the territory of another Member State and whereas the principle of free movement within the Community does not imply merely that there should be no discrimination on the grounds of nationality but is a fundamental right of independent validity...

D. Whereas in some Member States homosexuals are barred from certain professions such as the armed forces, diplomatic service and the merchant navy,

E. Whereas, moreover, even in those Member States whose legislation does not treat homosexuality between adults as an offence, in reality discrimination is practised against homosexuals with regard to work (recruitment, career prospects), job security, housing, prison conditions, respect for private life, and the right to visit or have custody of children,

F. Whereas it is unacceptable that homosexuality should be the reason, whether manifest or not, for individual dismissals, as has happened in a number of well-known cases...

1. Points out that in the campaign against discrimination of all kinds it is impossible to ignore or passively to accept *de facto* or *de jure* discrimination against homosexuals;

2. Deplores all forms of discrimination based on an individual's sexual tendencies...

4. Urges the Member States to:

(a) abolish any laws which make homosexual acts between consenting adults liable to punishment,

(b) apply the same age of consent as for heterosexual acts, as recommended by the Parliamentary Assembly of the Council of Europe,

(c) ban the keeping of special records on homosexuals by the police or any other authority,

(d) reject the classification of homosexuality as a mental illness;

5. Calls on the Commission to:

(a) renew its efforts with regard to dismissals to ensure that, while bearing in mind the present situation of mass unemployment, certain individuals are not unfairly treated for reasons relating to their private life,

(b) submit proposals to ensure that no cases arise in the Member States of discrimination against homosexuals with regard to access to employment and working conditions,

(c) take steps to induce the WHO to delete homosexuality from its International Classification of Diseases;

6. Also calls on the Commission to:

(a) invite Member States to provide, as soon as possible, a list of all provisions in their legislation which concern homosexuals,

(b) to identify, on the basis of such lists, any discrimination against homosexuals with regard to employment, housing and other social problems by drawing up a report, pursuant to Article 122 of the EEC Treaty;

7. Lastly, instructs its Legal Affairs Committee to examine as soon as possible in what way differences between the laws of the various Member States with regard to the ban on homosexuality or the minimum age of consent constitute barriers to the right to freedom of movement and to freedom of establishment as an employee or self-employed person and, in so doing, also to indicate what Community measures might be applied to remove such barriers...

D'ANCONA REPORT *On Violence Against Women*, 11 June 1986 (OJ No C 176, 14. 7. 1986, p. 75):

'12. Calls urgently for the extension of the concept of non-discrimination in the relevant legislation or legislative provisions in order to cover both discrimination on the basis of sex or marital status and discrimination on the basis of sexual preference...'

PARODI REPORT *On the Fight Against Aids*, 26 May 1989 (OJ No C 158, 26. 6. 1989, p. 479-480):

'3. Calls on the Member States and the Commission, as appropriate, to take measures aimed at...
    — ensuring compliance with existing laws and measures against discrimination on the grounds of race, sex, sexual orientation etc...'

BURON REPORT *On the Community Charter of Fundamental Social Rights*, 22 November 1989 (OJ No C 323, 27. 12. 1989, p.46):

'6. Stresses, with a view to the completion of the internal market and to protecting the interests of all Community nationals, that it considers that priority should be given in the Charter and the action programme to...
    — the right of all workers to equal protection regardless of

their nationality, race, religion, age, sex, sexual preference or legal status...'

FORD REPORT *On Racism and Xenophobia*, 10 October 1990 (Document A3-195/90, 23 July 1990):

'Recommendation 35: That a convention be drafted on a common refugee and asylum policy building on the principles of the UN Convention on Refugees allowing all those threatened by persecution because of their political, religious or philosophical beliefs or convictions, or gender or sexual orientation, to benefit...'

Complaint Against the European Community

(Partial text — formal case only)

COMPLAINT TO THE COMMISSION OF THE EUROPEAN
COMMUNITIES CONCERNING NON-COMPLIANCE WITH
COMMUNITY LAW AND THE PURSUIT OF POLICIES OF
EXCLUSION AND DISCRIMINATION WHICH VIOLATE
FUNDAMENTAL HUMAN RIGHTS (89/C26/07)

Name of Complainant: Peter Tatchell
Nationality : British
Complaint To : The Commission of the European Communities

Formal Case to the European Commission

This complaint is to the Commission of the European Communities concerning its failure to ensure compliance with the principles and provisions of the Treaties of the European Community, and concerning its pursuit of policies of exclusion and discrimination in violation of its obligations to respect and uphold fundamental human rights.

It is brought as an individual action on my own behalf as a gay man, and also as an action on the collective behalf of the estimated 32 million lesbians and gay men living in the 12 member states of the European Community.

Throughout this submission, the term EC refers collectively to the institutions of the European Community, including the European Commission.

The basis of my complaint is as follows:

1) That the EC has acted in an arbitrary, unreasonable and discriminatory manner against myself as a gay man, and against other gay men and lesbians, by

   (a) failing to respect and affirm my human rights and fundamental freedoms as a homosexual person and discriminating

against me on the grounds of my sexuality in EC policies,
legislation and programmes;

(b) denying me equal treatment and protection against discrimination with respect to my homosexuality in the EC's
regulations, decisions, directives, recommendations and opinions;

(c) tolerating anti-homosexual discrimination in the member
states, which causes me mental stress and diminishes my freedom to choose where I live, work and travel.

2) That the EC's discrimination by default and omission constitutes a failure by the EC to comply with its legal obligations,
as enshrined in the EC Treaties, to protect and promote the
human rights of all citizens of the EC member states (including, by implication, lesbian and gay citizens such as myself)
and to remove all forms of discrimination which act as
impediments to the realization of the EC's objectives of
ensuring the free movement of people, the creation of a
barrier-free internal market, and the harmonization of the
laws of the member states.

3) That by refusing to include within the EC's policies, decisions,
recommendations, opinions, programmes, directives and
regulations a commitment to equality of treatment and protection against discrimination on the grounds of sexual
orientation, the EC has thereby reinforced and perpetuated
discrimination against myself and other gay men and lesbians,
and by so doing it has acted contrary to the principles
enshrined in the Preambles to the EC Treaties which legally
empower and require the EC to ensure respect for human
rights and fundamental freedoms and to take initiatives for (i)
the achievement of equality, liberty, and social progress, (ii)
the realization of closer relations, harmonious development
and common policies by the member states, and (iii) the
fulfilment of improved living and working conditions for all
the peoples living in the countries of the EC.

4) That by declining to outlaw discrimination on the grounds of
sexual orientation and to remedy the wide variations in
employment law pertaining to lesbians and gay men in the
different member states, the EC has thereby restricted the
ability of myself and other gay men and lesbians to move

freely around the EC and to freely choose our place of abode and employment; thereby acting contrary to the provisions embodied in the Articles of the EC Treaties which legally authorize and compel the EC to ensure the free movement of people, the creation of a barrier-free internal market, and the harmonization of the regulations of the member states.

5) That this failure to ensure equality for homosexual people contradicts the EC's own recognition (OJ No L 257/2, 19. 10. 1968, p. 475) that there can be no genuine freedom of movement within the EC unless this freedom of movement applies equally to all the people of all the EC member states without distinction (including distinctions on the basis of sexuality), and unless there is also genuine equality of legal treatment for all people throughout the member states (encompassing equality of treatment on the grounds of sexual orientation); and that so long as there are different laws with respect to homosexuality in different member states, lesbian and gay people will not feel able to exercise genuine freedom of movement and the EC will therefore not be able to realize one of its principle legal obligations, as set out in its Treaties.

6) That the gravity of these unjustifiable and prejudiced decisions by the EC is compounded by the EC's recommendations, opinions, decisions, directives, regulations and programmes to protect certain other categories of people suffering discrimination (such as women, children and adolescents, elderly persons, and the disabled), while wilfully denying myself and other gay men and lesbians similar anti-discrimination protection.

7) That the adverse consequences of the EC's failure to ensure that Community law is applied to protect my rights as a gay man, and the rights of other gay men and lesbians, will be severely exacerbated by the creation of the Single European Market which will open up new employment opportunities and increase the mobility of labour; thereby exposing myself and other gay men and lesbians to greater risks of discrimination if our work requires us to travel or relocate in certain other EC countries, as the following examples illustrate:

(a) Whereas in the United Kingdom I have a legal right to have sexual relations with other consenting men over the age of 21, if I was posted to work in Ireland, where male homosexuality is still totally illegal, I would face a maximum penalty of life imprisonment for such relationships and up to ten years gaol for mere attempted homosexual acts.

(b) Should I decide to take advantage of the Single European Market and go to work in France, I would enjoy legal protection against discrimination in employment on account of my homosexuality; though if I subsequently returned to the United Kingdom, where no such legal protection exists for lesbians and gay men, I would immediately lose this anti-discrimination protection and be once again vulnerable to being denied employment and promotion and to being harassed or dismissed on the grounds of my sexual orientation.

(c) Likewise, were the new job openings resulting from the creation of the Single European Market to take me to certain other EC member states, such as Denmark and the Netherlands, I would be automatically entitled, as a resident of those countries, to a wide range of human rights and civil liberties which are denied to me as a gay man in the United Kingdom. These include the right to have a partnership with a person of the same sex recognized and protected by law, the right to take legal action to stop any public incitement of hatred or violence against me on the grounds of my sexual orientation, and the right to view sexually explicit homosexual-themed books, magazines and films which depict and celebrate my sexual orientation and lifestyle. If I returned to the United Kingdom at the end of my work contract, I would immediately forfeit all these civil and human rights, as would lesbian and gay citizens from other EC countries on entering the United Kingdom for work or leisure.

8) That as a result of the EC's non-compliance with its legal obligation to protect the rights of everyone equally and without distinction and to ensure the free movement of people and the establishment of an obstacle-free internal market without discrimination, myself and other gay men and lesbians are being denied equal rights under EC law; our freedom to live, work and travel within the EC is severely diminished; and the EC's failure to remedy these grievances

violates and undermines the human rights and dignity, freedom of choice and quality of life, employment and income opportunities, residential and recreational options, public respect and social esteem, and the psychological and emotional well-being of myself and other gay men and lesbians in the 12 member states.

9) That the European Commission must therefore publicly commit itself to take swift and effective action to remedy these violations, discriminations and omissions against myself and other gay men and lesbians, including the following initiatives:

(a) A commitment to recognize and protect the human rights and fundamental freedoms of lesbians and gay men in all appropriate present and future EC proposals, recommendations, opinions, directives, programmes, decisions and regulations (particularly those concerning the workplace and social and human rights), based on an official acceptance of the principle that homosexual people are entitled to 'full equality in law' and to 'legal protection against discrimination'.

(b) A commitment to include proposals for the protection of lesbian and gay employees against all aspects of workplace discrimination on the grounds of sexual orientation within the next Action Programme for the implementation of the Community Charter of the Fundamental Social Rights of Workers.

(c) A commitment to recommend to the member state governments, and to the Council of Ministers, the amendment of the EC Treaties to ensure an explicit legal remit for action on social and human rights issues, including issues of sexuality, and to ensure future equality and anti-discrimination initiatives to be undertaken by the EC to harmonize the laws of the 12 member countries with respect to the rights of lesbians and gay men, based on the most progressive and enlightened practice in the countries concerned.

Signed: Peter Tatchell Dated: 1 July 1991

Also by Peter Tatchell

AIDS: A GUIDE TO SURVIVAL

In this radical self-help manual for understanding, preventing and fighting back against Aids, Peter Tatchell brings a welcome message of hope for the many people already exposed to the HIV virus. By fighting back mentally and physically, people with the virus can reduce their chance of developing Aids, and even those who already have the disease can improve their prospects of survival.

This book sets out a comprehensive programme for strengthening the body's natural defences by means of diet, exercise, sleep and relaxation methods. It explains how to fight Aids psychologically, using meditation and mental imagery, and pays special attention to sustaining self-valuation and the will to live.

"A fundamentally important book…provides hope where previously there was none" — *City Limits*

"Tatchell's practical approach, contempt for fatalism and self-pity, and advocacy of the afflicted's self-activity, are surely right" — *The Listener*

"This is the fight-back book." — *Time Out*

UK £4.95   US $8.95

GMP books can be ordered from any bookshop in the UK, and from specialised bookshops overseas. If you prefer to order by mail, please send full retail price plus £1.50 for postage and packing to:

GMP Publishers Ltd (GB),
P O Box 247, London N17 9QR.

For payment by Access/Eurocard/Mastercard/American Express/Visa, please give number and signature.

A comprehensive mail-order catalogue is also available.

In North America order from Alyson Publications Inc.,
40 Plympton St, Boston, MA 02118, USA.

In Australia order from Bulldog Books,
P O Box 155, Broadway, NSW 2007, Australia.

Name and Address in block letters please:

Name
_____

Address
_____

_____

_____

_____